Victorian Cakes

Caroline B. King

Victorian Cakes

A REMINISCENCE
WITH
RECIPES

By Caroline B. King
With an Introduction by Jill Gardner

ARIS / BERKELEY

LC 86-1204

ISBN 0-943186-26-9

Aris Books are published by
Harris Publishing Company, Inc.
1621 Fifth Street
Berkeley, CA 94710
(415) 527-5171

Book trade distribution by Simon and Schuster
a division of Simon & Schuster, Inc.
Simon & Schuster Building, Rockefeller Center
1230 Avenue of the Americas, New York, NY 10020

Cover and book design by Linda Lane

First printing, March 1986
10 9 8 7 6 5 4 3 2 1
Manufactured in the United States of America

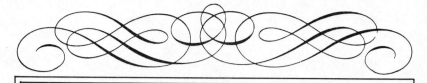

$\mathcal{C}$ontents

To Grace

Whose childhood demands for stories
" 'bout when you were little," served
to keep alive and green, the memory
of my youth.

❧

Before making the desserts in *Victorian Cakes*, please
refer to the section, About the Recipes. Jill Gardner
has tested all the recipes and offers information on
ingredients and techniques that will help insure success.

Introduction

In the 1880s, the era about which *Victorian Cakes* is written, Victorian sensibilities ruled the cultures of England and America. On both sides of the Atlantic, the decorum of everyday living was reflected in the ponderous elegance and carefully prescribed dining rituals of the rising middle class. To the Victorians, home and family were a microcosm of God's domain, and the kitchen was the center of that tiny world. Above all else, Victorians loved good things to eat. Every prosperous Victorian matron saw to it that a lavish array of rich dishes crowded across her table. She could produce, if the occasion demanded it, that hallmark of Victorian cuisine (and epitome of Victorian understatement): the trifle.

Victorian housewives regularly consulted their copies of Mrs. Beeton's *Book of Household Management*. By the close of the nineteenth century, cookbooks had become an integral part of a bride's trousseau, and Mrs. Beeton had become the final arbiter on all issues relating to the preparation and serving of food. Mrs. Beeton was absolutely certain that a servant girl, or even a cook, was present in every well-run household. And in Victorian America, a stout, strong-armed "hired girl" (sometimes two) became a necessary status symbol. The beating, whisking and stirring called for by Mrs. Beeton, Mrs. Lincoln, Maria Parloa, and all the other cookery writers of the time might well tax today's electric mixers.

The subject of Victorian cookbooks is fascinating. My tattered, soft-bound edition of *Cassell's Half-dollar Cookbook*, "the largest and most comprehensive work on the subject of cookery ever published for a shilling," devotes seventy-three pages of very small print to dessert puddings. In the preface of the book, the editor maintains that "the secret of good cooking is *economy*." While the recipe for Norfolk dumplings—individual puddings of store-bought muffins boiled in water for twenty minutes ("they will swell considerably") and served with a sweet sauce—is economical *in extremis,* Nesselrode pudding is a typically rich and luxurious Victorian molded dessert of fresh lemon peel- and vanilla-scented chestnut puree, sugar, maraschino liqueur, thick cream, currants, candied fruit and a bit of gelatin.

Literally a dime a dozen, the Victorian pamphlet cookbooks advertised everything from flour and other baking products to life insurance and patent medicine. I have a drawer full of these fancifully illustrated recipe collections. The cover of *The Rumford Almanac Cookbook of 1888* is adorned with a cherubic boy-child, all curly locks and white lace bib, in the style of a baby Fauntleroy. Among the miscellany of information included in the book are directions for arriving at the proper oven temperature for baking—throw a spoonful of flour on the floor of the oven; if the oven is at the correct temperature, the flour will turn a brownish-yellow in five or ten seconds—and testimonials to the excellence of Rumford products—"Miss Parloa, of the famous Boston Cookery School, says: 'I have used your baking preparations with perfect success, for bread, biscuit and cake.' "

Mrs. Lincoln's *Frozen Dainties* cookbook, published by the White Mountain Freezer Company, contains "fifty choice recipes" for ice creams, ices and other frozen desserts. The success of Mrs. Lincoln's recipes is guaranteed unconditionally only if a White Mountain ice cream freezer is employed in the making of the "frozen dainties." Printed on heavy, glossy paper, this pamphlet cookbook is beautifully illustrated with highly decorative drawings of fruits, flowers and Victorian maidens. The helpful cookery hints given at the bottom of each page, although pleasant, are hardly profound, for instance: "Serve wafers, fancy crackers or sponge cake with ice cream" and "One tablespoon of gelatin is as much as you can pile up compactly in a tablespoon," but the recipe for chocolate ice cream is tantalizingly rich. To a base of rich custard, two melted bars of sweetened vanilla chocolate are added, along with a good pinch of Ceylon cinnamon.

Many a Victorian cookbook focused on sweets. Charlottes, pastries, cakes, molded creams and glaces, in all shapes and sizes, were the *chefs d'oeuvre* at all prosperous Victorian tables. Desserts were romantic. "There is poetry in the dessert," said Mrs. Beeton, and what delighted the Victorians more than romance?

Ever since I first began reading about the pleasures of the Victorian table (did I start with Mrs. Beeton? I don't remember), I have collected Victorian cookbooks, particularly dessert cookbooks. *Victorian Cakes* is my overwhelming favorite. It is not a Victorian cookbook in the strictest sense, for Caroline B. King wrote this memoir of her Victorian childhood when she was seventy-six. But Mrs. King never bid good-bye to her Victorian past, where pleasures were of a simpler sort and to be found in the rhythms of daily living. *Victorian Cakes* is a portrait of Victorian life at its most delightful moments—particularly those spent in the kitchen and dining room. When the book was first published in 1941, its single printing yielded only 1,530 copies. I have an original edition of *Victorian Cakes,* and although it is dilapidated and the cover falling off, I treasure it greatly, for once inside the pages of the book I find myself with startling immediacy in another world: transplanted to a Chicago family in the 1880s.

There is Mother, who met and fell in love with her Irish husband-to-be when he was sent on business to her tiny Canadian hometown of Lake Erie. Fresh from Mrs. Apple's Finishing School for Young Ladies, this daughter of General Warren of the Canadian Army married Robert Campion. The two settled in Chicago, where he opened a law office and started a wholesale hardware concern. After the Chicago fire burnt the Campion's first home, Father moved his large family—which by then included five daughters—to the village of Lake View, the present Lincoln Park area of Chicago.

In good old Victorian fashion, Mother's elderly Aunt Sophie and Uncle George made their home with the Campions. Uncle George was a poet whose verse extolled the Empire Parlor Bedstead, the world's first folding bed, in daily newspaper advertisements. Uncle George's other claim to fame was his portrait, entitled "Life's Autumn," which hung in Chicago's first world's fair in 1893, the World's Columbian Exposition. (Visitors to the fair, "the grandest spectacle of modern times," encountered Edison's Kinetoscope, a ten-ton Canadian cheese, Venus de Milo molded in chocolate, Uncle George posing beside his portrait, and other such wonders.) Aunt Sophie, gentle, fat and rather deaf, possessed a romantic nature still; she was happiest when, reminiscing about the daily life of her youth, she would prepare the rich cakes and other desserts popular in that bygone time. All of Aunt Sophie's cakes had stories attached to them. My favorite is the story of the Dream Gingerbread Cake, so named because her mother "made the cake in a beautiful dream one night, and waking, was so impressed by the quality of her dream cake that then and there she flew to her kitchen in her nightcap and gown and made a cake exactly like the one in her dream."

Emily, Maud, Molly, Caroline and Kitty were the Campion daughters. Emily was "cakemaker in chief" and, being the eldest, blazed a path wherever she went, including the kitchen. Family and friends regularly paid tribute to Emily's extravagant layer cakes, rich with fruits and spices and swathed in shining icing. Emily could be quite unconventional. It was she who began the trick of substituting Mother's best perfume, Violet, Jockey Club or New Mown Hay (it was decided that Rose tasted like hair oil), for the flavoring in the family's heirloom recipe for Vanity Cake. The resulting Perfume Cake "was eaten with a certain delightsome awe by all who knew its secret." Maud was the only Campion endowed with naturally curly hair—a most important asset to a Victorian female—and accordingly, she was more mindful of appearances. Maud's culinary efforts reflected the most stylish creations of the era, including the new and popular Devil's Food and Angel Food Cakes. ("Paper towels!" exclaimed Father when he first tasted a piece of Angel Food Cake. He was a devotee of butter cakes.) Molly, the middle sister, was general assistant in the baking efforts; Caroline and the baby of the family, Kitty, spent hours hanging over mixing bowls and begging for an opportunity to help in the preparation of their sisters' sweet creations.

Anna, the "perenially young and blossomy" hired girl, shared with the rest of the family a predilection for licking the bowls and other utensils used in cake-making. Anna's German background provided the recipes for the Campion's elaborate Christmas baking: *Lebkuchen, Anis Plätzchen, Honigkuchen, Braunschweiger* and *Springerles.* Straight from Germany to the Campion household had come Emil the hired man, who took care of the chickens and the cow, tended the garden, kept the horses and drove

Father to the city. Anna and Emil were considered proper family members; when they announced their intention to marry, the Campion sisters were thrilled to find romance "existing in our kitchen, right under our very noses as it were."

In *Victorian Cakes*, Caroline B. King has written a series of autobiographical sketches of Chicago home-life in the 1880s and 1890s. Punctuating the charming tales of the domestic doings of the Campion household are mouthwatering descriptions of the old-fashioned and new-fashioned cakes dear to Victorian hearts. The recipes given in the book require a lavish amount of butter, sugar, eggs and cream, but Mrs. King writes that in the last decades of the nineteenth century, these ingredients "were mere commodities to be used in whatever quantities seemed good and reasonable, with no vexatious warnings of conscience or fears of shrinking budgets to hamper one's best efforts."

Of the seventy-odd cakes she has collected, I especially like the anecdotes about the Christmas fruitcakes. Work on these special cakes began the afternoon after Thanksgiving when the entire female corps of the family would slice and shell and sliver by hand the fruits and nuts and candied peel needed to produce four rich and succulent fruitcakes. The next morning, two different batters—one dark and one light, but both highly odorous of sherry— were assembled and poured into paper-lined tube pans, then slowly baked for several hours. The finished cakes were well-laved with more sherry or French brandy before being wrapped in old table linen and stored in stone crocks with sweet apples placed beside them. On Christmas Eve, when Emily unwrapped the cakes from their perfumed shrouds and thickly coated them with royal icing, "they did look wonderfully beautiful, something like snow-capped mountains. Delicate, thin slices of each fruitcake were alternately arranged in the Campion's treasured silver cake basket, which was given the place of honor at the Christmas tea table.

What endears this Christmas reminiscence to me is the mention of the silver cake basket. I have my own Victorian cake basket, given to me by my grandmother; I am looking at it now, and even empty of the fancy cakes and sweetmeats, which it is intended to display, there is still much to be admired. Bunches of grapes and their leafy vines twine around its heavy silver handle, which balances upright in an arc over the shallow, oval basket, fluted within and rimmed with a similar viniferous border. Only when dinner is an Event and the dessert is appropriate does my cake basket make a well-polished appearance. In Victorian times, the lovely silver baskets were daily appurtenances of the dining room where they gleamed, if not from the dinner or tea table, then from a prominent place on the sideboard.

In my mind's eye, I can see the dining room of the Campion home: the imposingly long, walnut table and matching sideboard are set for an evening party. Emily's magnificent Fig Cake, its four luscious layers richly filled and heaped high with a gleaming almond- or lemon-flavored white icing, rises from the center of the table on a footed, crystal cake stand. On either side, two tall silver epergnes display the best fruits of the season; apples, pears, peaches and plums are arranged in pyramids and draped with ruby and greenish-gold bunches of grapes. Stretching the length of the table, an amazing array of mouth-watering cakes wait to be cut. A rainbow-tinted Harlequin Cake, filled with lemon honey of a brilliant yellow hue, hides its variegated beauty under a decoration of pink sugar. The icing on Maud's Devil's Food Cake is embellished with halved walnuts. A hoar-frost of freshly grated coconut covers the top and sides of the new and very stylish White Mountain Cake. There is also a Ribbon Cake, an elegant creation of two kinds of cake—one lemon flavored and the other fragrant with citron and spices—layered with bright red jelly and extravagantly iced and decorated. Tiny crystal vases of flowers, placed here and there among the cakes, add to the beauty of the table.

On the sideboard, along with the champagne glasses and silver coffee service, the cake basket holds tiny jewel-like Madeleine Cakes. In a cut-glass bowl, cubes of glowing jelly decorate the Tipsy Parson, Aunt Sophie's version of trifle. To create this party dessert, a Madeira-soaked sponge cake is studded with almonds and mounded with currant jelly, rich custard and whipped cream.

Of course, this culinary equivalent of a Fourth-of-July fireworks display was reserved for company—cakes served at family meals were of a simpler, more "homey" nature. Applesauce Cake, "a mid-Victorian invention," had several variations, one of which the Campions ate hot from the oven as a sort of pudding dessert, topped with hard sauce. Father and Uncle George were partial to caraway-flecked Seed Cake, an invariable offering at every Victorian tea, while fresh Blackberry Cake with brown-sugar frosting appealed to everyone. One, Two, Three, Four Cake calls for one cup butter, two cups sugar, three cups flour and four eggs. Because its formula was so easy to remember and it could be flavored in any number of ways, One, Two, Three, Four Cake became the standard birthday cake in most nineteenth-century households, the Campions' included. (Baked in a loaf pan, this cake is superb when aged a day or two, then sliced and served with jam for tea. I recommend the addition of a cup of currants.)

How delicious are those memories of cakes enjoyed a century ago! I can almost smell the fragrance of Mother's Sweet Rusks and taste Susie's Maple Shortcake in its bath of heavy cream, the rich biscuit oozing butter and sandwiched with a thick layer of soft maple sugar. Nearly fifty years have passed since *Victorian Cakes* was written, but as with most authors whose books describe the smell and taste of good things to eat, no generation gap exists between Mrs. King and her readers.

I have been a fan of Mrs. King ever since I first came across a copy of *Victorian Cakes*. (In the basement of a college library that had seen better days, this delightful volume was buried in a dusty bin of other, quite ordinary cookbooks.) Mrs. King died in 1948, yet she is still remembered by former readers of *Country Gentleman* as that magazine's renowned women's editor. She was a protegee of Cyrus Curtis, whose publishing empire at one time included *Country Gentleman, The Saturday Evening Post, Ladies Home Journal*, the *Philadelphia Press*, and the *New York Evening Post*. Mrs. King wrote for many of the Curtis publications, and for all the leading women's magazines of her day, often writing under the pseudonym of Katherine Campion. Cookery and cookery writing were both her hobby and profession. In the early 1920s, after travelling around the United States collecting information and recipes, she produced a series of articles for *Ladies Home Journal* on regional American cooking. She also liked to garden, and her two books on gardening, *Rosemary Makes a Garden* and *This Was Ever in My Dream*, are pleasant *and* practical reading.

Mrs. King once wrote a whimsical account of her life in terms of the stoves she had encountered. There was the old iron giant with its lily decorations, so often mentioned in *Victorian Cakes*. Later came "the Happy Rover" portable stove which she and her husband used during the years they homesteaded on the Camas Prairie in Idaho (where Mrs. King taught home economics to the Nez Perce Indian women). No stove is mentioned, however, for the short period when, after the death of her husband, she returned to Chicago and supported herself and her two young daughters by selling McCormick vanilla to the rural housewives of Northern Illinois—driving from farm to farm in a horse-drawn buggy.

When she became women's editor of the *Philadelphia Press*, she was often asked to lecture on food preparation. At the outbreak of World War I, the subject was "food will win the war." The stoves she had to contend with were a motley collection:

"How I toiled and what stoves I encountered! Sometimes I would bake my war bread in a hastily erected stove in a church basement, or teach cold pack canning on a very unstable cooking apparatus in a shop window on a busy street. Once in a lodge hall I was put to it to bake a delicate pudding in an oven from which the door was missing, another time when the lesson included a puffy omelet I had to mix my ingredients in a school room and carry them across the street to cook them on a drugstore hot plate. I have never forgotten the time when a large and important flour mill invited me to bake before a critical audience of good housewives and I was obliged to place my precious batters in the pans in the auditorium, and hand them over to a little helper who in turn carried them to some mysterious spot in the mill to be baked. That experience taught me a lesson in faith that was very good for my soul."

In 1917, Mrs. King was appointed Head Army Dietician and sent to France for the duration of the war. "Army stoves were strange affairs," she wrote. "Ours were sunk in the red tinted mud so deep that one must also sit on the ground to operate them, and when it rained it was necessary to cover the stovepipe with a trench hat in order to keep the fire burning, or if it blew gales as it often did, someone had to hold the stovepipe in place. But dinner was always on time and fairly good, too." Mrs. King's granddaughter tells me that her grandmother often played Robin Hood to the hospitalized soldiers. With a small

French boy and his wagon as her accomplice and under the protection of darkness, she would climb through a window in the officer's mess hall and steal fruit, relaying oranges and whatever else she could find through the window to the boy, who would pile his wagon with the stolen booty. They then would drag the wagon to the hospital where Mrs. King would quarter the oranges and squeeze the juice into the mouths of the badly wounded.

Upon returning home from the war, Mrs. King built herself a small house outside of Philadelphia. A plethora of stoves followed until "at last, the stove to end all stove problems, my electric range in my modernized up-to-the-last-minute electric kitchen, glistening white with glowing color accents, and possessing every gadget under the sun to make my cooking an even more fascinating hobby."

Mrs. King wrote *Victorian Cakes* in that kitchen; in a sense, her life had come full circle. I wonder what she would think of kitchens today, designed with the high-tech efficiency of the computer age. I know she would regret the passing of the most important prerequisite of good cooking—patience. Few people seem to have enough time these days to prepare, serve, eat and properly enjoy a good meal, whether elaborate or deliciously simple. Yet, the Victorian amenities of living still exercise a hold on the late twentieth-century imagination, particularly those related to the pleasures of the table. In Victorian times, dessert was the climax of a meal, the *raison d'etre* of dinner. *Victorian Cakes* is not only a treasury of nineteenth-century America's favorite desserts, it provides a glimpse of the romance of dining in the Victorian Age.

Jill Gardner

Kitchen Fragrances

SOMETIMES, on my very busiest days, my bandbox kitchen all set for a morning of intensive baking, scientifically correct beaters and mixers and regulators just awaiting the flick of my finger to be at their whirling and whizzing, and time altogether too precious to be spent daydreaming—sometimes, on just such a morning, a whiff of heliotrope sweetness from the vanilla bottle or a breath of oriental fragrance from a spice can will send me far, far away. In a trice I'm back in the familiar casual old kitchen of my childhood, beating eggs on a huge cracked turkey platter, or measuring sugar or flour in a gigantic coffee cup which, having lost its handle, is no longer fit to appear in the polite society of the breakfast table.

It's a bustling place, that shabby, cozy old kitchen of ours, on a morning like this, and a fascinating place, too, even for a girl of twelve or thereabouts. There in the place of honor stands the chief actor in the morning's affairs, the heavy iron stove beaming under its coat of fresh polish which Anna, our hired girl, has applied by dint of elbow grease. Anna's strong hands have also brought the sheaf of nickel-plated calla lilies which decorates the oven door to a state of dazzling splendor, raked the ashes from the grate, and coaxed the fire to that glowing complexion which to

1

Mother means a "steady oven," just right for the generous cakes and loaves that will shortly be entrusted to its keeping.

Anna at the kitchen sink, washing endless pans and bowls, spoons and forks, is sturdy, red-armed, and pleasant of countenance. She is at peace with the whole world, as well she may be, having finished a bountiful breakfast that ended with twelve whacking pancakes steeped in fresh butter and brown-sugar sirup. Furthermore, she is already enjoying in anticipation the surreptitious tastes and occasional licking of bowls and mixing spoons when the cakemaking begins in good earnest. No matter how many times she may have to empty and refill her dishpan, or how many times she will have to scour with soap and sand, the old black iron sink and the pine drainboards that flank it, Anna is happy. Saturday is her big day, beginning with her early morning struggle with kindling wood and coal hod, and ending only when the mountains of supper dishes, washed rinsed and polished with snowy, sweet-smelling towels, are set away in their own special cupboards, and she and Henry, or whatever the current hired man's name may be, take the old Democrat wagon and set out for Anna's home on Clybourne Avenue. It is usually Sunday morning before they return, for the evening is bound to close with a dance and Anna arrives home, worn but jubilant, her shoes dangling over her arms from their long laces, to rake ashes, polish the stove, and begin breakfast preparations.

I can't picture the old kitchen without seeing Anna, perennially young and blossomy washing dishes at the kitchen sink, or scrubbing the immaculate white pine table, Mother s pride and our vexation, for never a drop of any soilful thing must mar its dazzling purity. Candy pulls, Halloween frolics, even the spreading of jelly on slices of bread, were taboo, if in any way the cherished table must be involved. But Anna often washed the supper dishes on its spotless surface, especially if we youngsters could be coaxed by promises of fairy tales to help dry them, for the table, being of noble proportions, afforded space for several helpers to set cups and plates as they were finished. To us Anna was Grimm Brothers, Hans Christian Andersen, and half a dozen other famous storytellers rolled into one. Her glowing descriptions of kings' palaces and queens' gowns make me realize now what a marvelous decorator or *couturière* was lost to the world when Anna decided to go to work in Mother's kitchen.

Until Emil's advent, we never found much to interest us in the hired men who came and went, for they were all birds of passage. Mother declared Father spoiled them, for no sooner had they shown some ability and willingness to help about the house than Father managed to discover potential business aptitude in them and soon had them working in his office, and then of course we never saw them again. Emil came to us direct from Germany, a funny little figure carrying all his worldly possessions in a bright-hued bandanna handkerchief and a gaudy carpetbag. Emil had no leanings toward law or business and so remained a simple hired man, to Anna's great contentment, for she too, was German, and Emil was immediately taken into her family's fold and affections, and became an honored guest at all the Clybourne Avenue social gatherings.

Emil milked the cow, tended the garden and the chickens, drove Father into the city, kept the horses (and we had several) shining like satin and their harness and trappings like patent leather and silver, scoured the knives, filled and cleaned the kerosene lamps, and in his spare time made himself obligingly useful about the house. Anna and Emil were very important members of our household, and we all loved and respected them. Certainly I can not picture the old kitchen without them, or more especially without Anna, and I think life would have lost much of its zest for her had those stupendous Saturday morning bakings ever ceased.

What cakes that old lily-garnished stove did turn out! Sometimes I think no modern cake, however scientifically planned and skillfully put together, can ever quite equal those cakes of the eighties, when butter and eggs and cream were mere commodities to be used in whatever quantities seemed good and reasonable, with no vexatious warnings of conscience of fears of shrinking budgets to hamper one's best efforts.

Butter at thirty cents a pound was considered dear. Its normal price was twenty or twenty-five cents, so we measured generously even when a receipt demanded a whole cupful; and as to our measuring cups, they just happened. Our old handleless coffee cup would, compared to present standards, appear like a young bowl.

We bought eggs for fifteen cents a dozen when our own hens were not laying. Sometimes in winter the price rose to twenty- five cents, never more. They were twenty-five cents, or there were no eggs, and then we made "no egg" cakes and good ones too. Sponge cake was leavened to an ethereal lightness with eggs; and pound cake, rich, fine-textured, deeply golden, emitting entrancing whiffs of lemon and mace, also called for eggs in generous numbers.

Our kitchen, as I recall it, was of magnificent proportions, compared to the pocket-sized workshops we call kitchens today. It was cheery and bright, with many windows which looked out on Mother's flower beds, brilliant with color for at least six months of the year. During the remaining months wire plant stands filled with geraniums, heliotrope, fuchsias, and sometimes calla lillies, occupied most of the window space. The pine-board floor, sand-scrubbed many times a week, always gave forth a clean fresh scent of resin and yellow soap.

In addition to the great worktable that Mother prized so highly, there were other smaller but equally white tables, and the flour barrel, neatly topped with the pastry board, afforded a resting place for the large japanned bread-box which received its weekly scrubbing and airing in the sunshine to be pure and sweet for Mother's fresh loaves and light rolls when the oven had baked them to just that nut-brown tint that meant perfection to Father.

The cupboard stretched the entire length of one end of the room, and from its doors, always slightly ajar, stole forth, in a never-to-be-forgotten effluvium, good smells of so many sorts and descriptions that even to think of them today makes me overwhelmingly homesick.

The kitchen clock had its permanent position on one wall of the kitchen and occupied an important place in the daily lives of each one of us, for it not only announced the time of day, the day of the month, and the year, but also foretold the weather so accurately that my father would not have dreamed of starting to the city without consulting it, any more than he would have gone without his green bag or his hat. A map of England flanked the clock on one side, and in smaller size and less colorfully portrayed, a map of the United States on the other. Kerosene lamps in green-painted iron brackets lighted the work tables, the sink, and the stove. Above the great pine table the pewter hot-dish covers, tin and copper saucepans, ladles and strainers, were conveniently hung and once a week received their scouring with soap and sand.

It was a cheery kitchen, immaculate but never painfully orderly, because of too constant use, for there was never a moment in the day, I believe, that some sort of activity was not in progress within its four walls. Bread baking was an almost daily occurrence. Mother made her bread by the old time-honored sponge method, setting it after supper one day and baking it in the early afternoon of the day following. Preserving carried on from late May, when the rhubarb in the garden was ready for the jam pots, until Halloween, when the last green tomatoes, salvaged from the frosted vines, were transformed into a sort of rich marmalade with an exotic East Indian flavor that was very exciting. All through June I helped hull strawberries and pit cherries, with my book opened beside me at the piece I was to speak on the last day of school, so that Longfellow and Whittier, both favorites of my teachers, became so associated with strawberries and cherries that I could scarcely think of one without the other.

Vacation meant raspberry jam and currant jelly, lunch under the trees for us children, bread-and-butter sandwiches with layers of the fresh, hot sweet spread thickly between, and ice-cold milk in shining tin mugs. How marvelously tempting the old kitchen would smell when we brought in our plates and cups!

In September I would come home from school in the late afternoon to find peach marmalade side by side with a kettle of rich vegetable soup, such as only Mother could make, simmering on the back of Anna's spotless stove. A bowl of soup, a thick slice of Mother's fresh bread piled with the hot marmalade, and I was fortified until suppertime, and ready for my afternoon tasks, one of which was to prepare Alice's evening repast.

Alice was our cow, and Father was as particular about her meals as Mother was about our own. Emil was not to be trusted with their preparation any more than Anna was permitted to make our bread; these important duties were to be performed only by members of the family, and the preparation of Alice's six o'clock mash fell to my lot. I think I rather enjoyed it, however, as I did any sort of mixing and stirring.

Through a chute from the bin in the loft, I would half

fill a large, scrupulously clean cedar pail with bran. Then I must add a quart of what Father called "shorts" and a handful of salt. Over this mixture I poured a kettle of boiling water; and when this had cooled sufficiently, I stirred the mash thoroughly and carefully with my hands until it resembled a pudding; then it was ready. Later more water would be added, warm if the weather were cool, cold in summer, for Father believed his cow enjoyed her comfortable meal as well as he did his own.

My other chores were not so pleasant. An hour's practice on the piano was one of them, and woe betide me if, in the evening, I had to reply to Father's stern, "Have you practiced today?" with a whispered "No, sir."

Polishing Father's extra pair of high boots, which he removed in the evenings with the aid of a boot-jack, was my job also. Emil would willingly have relieved me of this task; but, as it was my one source of income, I clung to it zealously, and every Saturday night, if Father did not forget, I received my precious silver dime and was rich and envied for at least an hour.

Even more fascinating than the kitchen with all its gay bustle and good smells was the milk room, with its safes filled with deep pans of rich milk; jars of thick cream waiting to be whipped into Devonshire butter (one of Mother's specialties); crocks of green-tomato pickles with mustard seed and slivers of silvery onions adding their pungency; spiced peaches in wide-mouthed gallon jars of clear glass; ginger pears, favorite sweetmeats for cold Sunday night suppers, eaten with hot buttered toast and liberal helpings of Mother's clotted cream; boxes of raisins in luscious layers; preserved citron; a certain cheese Father adored, always well moistened with port wine; smoked meats and fish; a ham, usually boiled or baked and ready for slicing; jars of cookies, some with caraway seed for Father and Uncle George, others plain for us children;

doughnuts, and gingerbread. Always a nice selection, and often all these appetite tempters might be found behind the green wire doors of those mysterious safes.

Our icebox was of the old chest variety. You lifted the heavy lid and removed half the contents before you found the thing you were after, usually reposing snugly at the very bottom. Because of a large pan which caught the drip from the melting ice and had frequently to be emptied, the chest occupied a corner of the milk room conveniently near the kitchen door. Once or twice a week everything in the box was taken out and the chest given a thorough scouring and scalding, and the ice wrapped in many thicknesses of newspaper to make it last as long as possible.

The milk room was also Father's wine cellar. In a cupboard, to which he alone held the key, his supply of cherished liquors was stowed away—whiskey, Irish or Scotch, brandy in case of sickness, a bottle or two of port, a jug of sherry, a few cordials, and an assortment of sauternes, clarets, and Rhine wines, which he considered much more healthful dinner beverages than water. These wines were served in tall glasses with ice and sugar. Whether that was the Victorian fashion or merely my father's invention, I can not say, but they were very pleasant, especially, we children thought, after the melting ice had diluted them so that only a faint flavor and tartness remained.

Mother had her own sacred corner in the milk room also. Here she kept certain jars of pickled olives reserved for very unusual occasions and very special company. I call them pickled olives, for that is exactly what they were; they bore no resemblance whatever to our modern olives, and would not, I fear, appeal to the modern appetite.

Father often found it necessary to go to New York on some consultation or other business, and on his return he usually presented Mother with some novel or rare delicacy. One autumn his gift was a dozen quart jars of Spanish olives. Of course we children lost no time in sampling them. We immediately decided they tasted like tears. At that, Mother took a puzzled second taste and remarked reproachfully:

"Why, Robert, these olives have only been brined. They aren't finished. Too bad you bought such a lot of them."

But she was equal to the occasion, and in less than twenty-four hours all the olives reposed in a bath of spiced and sweetened vinegar which was renewed several times until no hint of tears remained.

In winter apples were stored in the milk room, which was slightly warmer than the cellar. We always had two barrels, one of sweet apples for eating and baking, the other of tart and juicy ones for pies and other cooking.

Father was known far and wide as a "good provider." He scorned buying in small lots. "Naught's worth of nothing in a paper bag," he termed such purchases. The springs of the old Democrat wagon were often hopelessly flattened with the weight of the boxes and barrels, jugs and demijohns, that almost hid him from sight as he turned into our lane at the end of his long drive home.

Then what busy and interesting evenings we would have stowing the good things away in the milk room and cellar! It was not much fun wrapping each apple in bits of newspaper, but even that could be accomplished without grumbling if Father were in a good humor, and if, as we worked, he would tell us tales of his boyhood in Ireland. If it were summer and his bacon proved to be strawberries or cherries, we would all sit round the kitchen table with its protecting cover of oilcloth, hulling or pitting with all our might. The climax of the event would be reached when Mother, having weighed the fruit, would cover it thickly with sugar, stirring it a bit, and then set it away to await further operations in the morning. But before it was finally

9

hidden from our sight, we would each receive a bountiful dishful, and although we had gorged ourselves as we worked, we devoured our treat with relish.

Our big commodious kitchen afforded space for several workers, and there on Saturday mornings one could always find Mother busy with great mountains of dough that later in the day, when the substantial old oven had received it in varying forms of loaves, rolls, bread, cake, and rusks, would send its devastating fragrance through the entire house to the very attic, where I usually retired to write my Monday composition. Later these delicacies would repose on the spotless table, wrapped and half-concealed beneath a threadbare damask tablecloth, once a prized possession, but now, much darned and mended by Aunt Sophie's deft hands, relegated solely to the use of the fresh baked bread.

The loaves were covered but not wholly hidden, for that would have sorely disappointed Father, who, when he returned from the city, tired and hungry, liked nothing better than to break the crust (he called it the heel) from an entire loaf or two, and munch it slowly and appreciatively, with a glass of cold buttermilk to wash it down, as he sat on the side porch and contemplated his currant bushes. Sometimes he studied a ponderous lawbook, and this, long after he had ceased to use it, retained dark buttery spots where bits of the rich crust had fallen as he ate. Naturally, Mother looked askance at this bread vandalism, but she used to say, while regarding her torn loaves sadly,

"Your Father works so hard and has so few pleasures."

As to pleasures I am not so sure, but work hard he did, for he had a huge family to feed and clothe—five growing daughters, often a ward or two, sons, of old schoolmates in Ireland or England, Uncle George and Aunt Sophie, and of course Anna and Tommy or Henry or

Emil. In addition there were dependents, droves of them, to whom he was always the squire or the lawyer, whose belief in him was boundless and who flocked to him to settle their difficulties, legal or financial, at every turn. There was Mary, the washerwoman, whose constantly increasing family ate three square meals in our summer kitchen every Monday and Tuesday while she rubbed our linen on the washboard and smoothed it with a flatiron. Mary was constantly on the verge of leaving her roving husband but she always meekly forgave him. There was Mrs. White, a hooked-nosed fighting little woman, who came at least once a week for free legal advice and anything in the line of clothing or provisions the lawyer's family might have to give her. Anna's family, too, looked upon him as a sort of all-the-year-round Kris Kringle; and then there were the Bergmans, who were constantly quarreling with their neighbors about the boundaries of their truck patch. Every one came to Father for advice and more substantial assistance, which he was always ready and willing to bestow.

And of course there was company, almost always there was company for Father and Mother enjoyed nothing quite so much as entertaining friends at their table. We children, too, although it meant our sleeping in the attic when they remained overnight, adored company. We welcomed each arrival with open arms, carried satchels and bags with cheerful zeal, filled heavy bedroom pitchers with rain water, set forth fresh-scented soap, draped towel racks with the best linen, and as a crowning touch, pierced in the pincushion on the bureau with bright new pins the initials of the lucky guest who was to enjoy all this elegance and comfort.

The dining room, darkened all day, was a gay sight when six o'clock arrived. There were extra leaves in the already long table to make it of even greater length. On the

best tablecloth, satin-smooth and shining, with the gleaming silver caster in the center and tight little bouquets from
the garden on either side, lay platters of cold boiled tongue;
thinly sliced lemon-flavored veal loaf (one of our homely
specialties); chicken salad; perhaps a pan of Mother's version of Saturday baked beans; jellies, gold, red and purple;
radishes and pickles; great puffy, feathery, hot rolls; cheese
under a delicate green glass dome on a carved ash platter.
The tea service stood before Mother, and pitchers of
creamy milk and buttermilk at the corners; and for dessert
we had fresh fruit with clotted cream in summer, floating
island or citron preserves in winter, with one of Emily's
famous cakes, which through the meal had reposed conspicuously, as though to sound a note of warning if appetites
might be proving overlusty on a high glass cake stand on
the walnut sideboard, with plates, dessert forks, and
spoons beside it.

Those cakes of my sister's! Were they larger or better
than those we bake today? Perhaps. Larger they must have
been to afford such satisfying slices as they did, with seconds all round on demand. But is it only my imagination
that makes them in retrospect seem more luscious, ten-
derer, finer textured, altogether delectable?

Our Daring Sister

$\mathcal{M}$OTHER MADE GOOD CAKES, sat-
isfying cakes, excellent for taking along in school lunch baskets and on holiday rambles in the woods, but Emily was
"cakemaker in chief" in our large household. I think she
was never so happy as on those busy Saturday mornings in
the kitchen when she could mix and beat and invent to her
soul's delight. Emily had her own table in the kitchen, her
own bowls and pans and wooden spoons and her very
own private cupboard where she kept her treasures—her
colors, extracts, and what not for flavoring and beautifying
her cakes.

She was a daring young woman, her daring extending
even into her cookery. As she was the oldest, she was not
required to obey all the rules set down for us younger children; but it was our private opinion that rules were relaxed
in her case because Father knew she would break them anyway. But how gay she made our lives, always thinking of
something different and sometimes a little dangerous to
do, something that, while it might entertain us mightily,
brought little shivers of delicious terror in its wake!

Frequently her daring took some form of entertaining
when many cakes would be demanded. Once she gave a
party when Father was away on some legal business, a

party, moreover, to which she invited *young men*—which was just not *done* in our home! If masculine guests were desired, Father would invite them, he explained, and often he did so, but his guests were not *young men*. Never!

On this occasion, the very moment his train had pulled safely out of the station, Emily, with the help of Maud, next in line and greatly in sympathy, harnessed Daisy and Dolly to the phaeton and started on the rounds of their friends' homes. They called on Sam Parkes, who could always be counted upon to recite anything from "Shamus O'Brien" to "Curfew Shall Not Ring Tonight"; Willie McAlister, who was very good at the piano, and his brother Tom; the Richardson boys; Charlie Cutter, Jack Pooley, and several others equally desirable, with their sisters if they had them; and a few other girls, Mattie Church, Clara Waterman, Mabel Lord, and so on.

"Tomorrow night at eight o'clock, and it's a Valentine party, don't forget," urged my sisters, and everybody gaily promised to be on hand.

The next day it rained, poured, descended in torrents but my sisters blithely prepared for the party A Valentine box was set up in the hall, where everyone who came was expected to deposit his or her sweet missives.

Emily and Maud spent the morning in the kitchen busily baking. Molly, our middle sister, was helper, messenger, and general all-round assistant. Mother protestingly boiled a tongue and made a tempting veal salad. Anna swept and garnished the front and back parlors, with Aunt Sophie doing her bit. Uncle George retired to the hayloft to write his daily poem. Emil, looking scared and doubtful, ran hither and thither, carrying, fetching, polishing, and sweeping. At last everything was ready. Emily had even made ice cream, flavoring it with Father's best sherry, though how she contrived to break into his wine closet we never knew.

The guests arrived, and soon the house, already bright with lights from coal-oil lamps in the crystal chandeliers, was gay with music and laughter. I remember there was even some dancing; supper was set forth in the dining room, the doors having remained closed until the proper moment. We two little ones who had been allowed to stay up for the festivities were wild with excitement. Emily's cheeks were scarlet, partly, perhaps, because she had rubbed them with petals from an artificial rose dipped in perfume. Maud's hair was curled in a multitude of ringlets, and Mother had fastened a gold filigree butterfly, quivering delicately on a wire spring, at one side. Molly wore a red surah blouse which set off her dark eyes and skin becomingly. Even Mother and Aunt Sophie had put on their silk dresses for the momentous occasion, though they both expressed their disapproval and Mother even scolded Emily quite roundly.

The time came to read the Valentine verses aloud, and Sam Parkes who had been selected for this ceremony, began. The rhymes were of course very sentimental, and he read them with gusto. All was going merrily, although outside the rain was coming down furiously, and the wind had risen to a perfect gale. But no one seemed to hear anything but Sam's voice as he rolled out the sweet nothings printed on the Valentines. Mother and Aunt Sophie, with large aprons over their silks, were making coffee and cutting cake, so they were not present when the front door opened suddenly and Father, his umbrella still wide open, stalked into the hall, then into the front parlor.

A very few words were spoken, and those definitely not of welcome. In five minutes every guest had gone on his or her homeward way. Anna and my sisters dashed cellarward with the cakes, Aunt Sophie went cowardly to bed, and to poor Mother was left the task of placating Father.

"Just a few young folks who dropped in casually," she explained, first making sure that all the refreshments were safely out of the way. "Some of the girls' high-school friends, surely no harm in that."

Father gave her just one look, and Mother withered like a seared rose, for in that look he had expressed his awareness of the silk dress, the coral jewelry, and the high French twist she had given her hair.

For several days we were all very quiet and obedient. Even Emily went about with a chastened look on her face, but that might have been caused by the fact that all her beautiful cakes were discovered floating in three feet of water in the cellar the next morning, along with cabbages, carrots, empty bottles, and the ice cream freezer, tipped on its side and half filled with dirty water.

It was very wonderful to watch Emily at her cake baking, and it was even more wonderful when I was elected to help her, which was not half as often as I would have liked. I adored beating eggs, buttering pans, and rubbing flour through the old flat sieve, and I also adored the tastes that occasionally came my way as my sister stirred and whipped and added flavoring drop by drop.

Unfortunately for me, there were three girls, all older and presumably more capable than I, so it was not often that good fortune came my way. Emily was about twenty, Maude eighteen, and Molly almost seventeen. I was twelve at this time and Kitty, the baby of the family, nine. Naturally I longed to be grouped with my older sisters, but in some way or other I never was. Kitty and I were youngsters and had to go to bed at nine o'clock. We were never allowed to do any of the exciting things that always seemed to happen after we were safely tucked away for the night. So it was not very likely that a grown-up young lady would permit a small sister of twelve to share her fascinating tasks unless there was positively no help for it.

Occasionally, however, when Maud had a music lesson to prepare before the arrival of strict old Professor Day in the early afternoon, Molly, who really detested cooking, would resign in my favor, and I would then become my eldest sister's helper. Feeling very important I would scrub my hands, tie back my long braids and follow Emily, whom I worshiped, to the kitchen. There, established at her especial table with all her treasured ingredients about her, she would turn out one of those superb cakes that in all these years I have never been able to equal.

Emily's equipment, compared to our modern tools, was poor and inadequate—pans which had seen many better days; an ironstone mixing bowl almost too heavy for her to lift, even with my assistance; a large cracked turkey platter with an old silver dinner fork for beating eggs; the gigantic coffee cup without a handle; and the flat hoop sieve through which the flour must be pushed by main force. For measuring soda or baking powder we used our various-sized everyday teaspoons. Extracts were added drop by drop, Emily and I tasting occasionally to assure ourselves that the flavor was never too strong or apparent. New equipment was never even suggested. In fact, we would not have wished to exchange our familiar utensils for any others, no matter how modern or handsome they might have been.

Emily made the morning's baking quite as interesting and exciting as she made everything else. From one source or another she had picked up a wonderful collection of facts on almost every subject under the sun, it seemed, and as we worked she would tell me romantic tales of spices, chocolate, coconut, and other commodities we happened to be using, never allowing her attention to wander dangerously far from the mixing and stirring and measuring. I often wonder now, when I think of these mornings in the cozy old kitchen, where she gained all this knowledge.

Her methods, too, were far in advance of my mother's, and there were not many cookery books in the early eighties, and none of them at all scientific. But Emily knew the whys and wherefores of cookery even as the experts know them today. When a delicate cake was planned, she would substitute two or three tablespoons of cornstarch for the same amount of flour to assure a finer texture, for we had but one grade of flour and that was always selected for its bread qualities. She brushed her baking pans with soft butter rather than drippings or other fats because, as she explained, "The crust of the cake is the part you taste first and butter is a flavor as well as a shortening." Then, to ensure a smooth, even surface for icing, she would deftly sprinkle a film of flour over the bottom and sides of the pan before the batter went into it. It was fascinating to watch her spoon in the velvety stuff, taking care that it was a little higher at the sides than in the middle, never dragging it over the surface, which would tend to make it stick, and giving the pan a few sharp taps on the table to prevent air bubbles and so on—all scientifically correct today, but Emily knew nothing of science, she was merely a very good cakemaker.

There was one cake, I recall, that always remained a mystery to our friends, who could never discover just what magic Emily used to produce so exquisite a flavor. But Vanity Cake would have been an exquisite cake no matter how it might be flavored, or in fact if it were left entirely unflavored. The recipe was a family heirloom, but the delicate fragrance and heavenly flavor were due entirely to the fact that Emily substituted lemon verbena sprigs for the usual extracts. On one occasion when I was permitted to bring teacher home for tea, the cake was flavored with real rose petals and masked with a delicate pink icing. I have never forgotten that ambrosial cake. Emily's receipt went as follows:

⟋ VANITY CAKE ⟍

½ cup of butter
1½ cups sugar
½ cup milk
6 egg whites
1½ cups flour

½ cup cornstarch
1½ teaspoons baking
   powder
Flavoring

The original receipt called for cream of tartar in place of baking powder, and Aunt Sophie and Mother still inclined to its use, but Emily was modern, for those days, and remodeled the receipt according to her own ideas. Her measurements were generous—we would call them rounding today—and she assembled the ingredients in the usual manner, creaming the butter in her bowl which had been first rinsed with warm water and carefully dried, adding the sugar and beating both together to the texture of whipped cream, whipping the egg whites to snowy peaks on the turkey platter, sifting flour, cornstarch, and baking powder together and adding them alternately with the milk, and finally folding in the egg whites with as little actual beating or stirring as possible. Emily introduced the flavoring in a unique way. After brushing her pans with soft butter, she would arrange lemon verbena leaves over the surface, then spoon in the batter, and bake the cake in her usual heedful way. When it was finished and turned from the pan, she would peel off the aromatic leaves, and ice the cake with a delicate icing faintly flavored with lemon.

Emily's Vanity Cake was a mysterious cake but very delicious. Perfume Cake was a sort of sport from Vanity Cake invented by our daring big sister and eaten with a certain delightsome awe by all who knew its secret, which was after all a simple one, merely that of substituting a few drops of Mother's best perfume for the usual vanilla or almond extract. "Violet" we thought made the best cake, though "New-Mown Hay" or even "Jockey Club" were acceptable. "Rose" we shunned, declaring it tasted like hair oil, but later when Emily discovered rosewater and used it with great discretion, we were converted.

Never a surprise party or a church supper or a social took place in our neighborhood that Emily was not besieged with requests for a Ribbon Cake. It was considered her specialty and very elegant, and I think she rather enjoyed the prestige the cake brought to her. Emily's Ribbon Cake was bound to make any affair a success, so far as food went. It was a fussy cake, this famous Ribbon Cake, and that may have been one reason why my sister so adored making it. When it was finished and stood proudly on the parlor table waiting to be escorted to the party, it was truly a grand cake, slightly oriental in its fragrant spiciness, and altogether alluring. Here is the way it was made:

RIBBON CAKE

First Part	Second Part
⅔ cup butter	1 large cup raisins, seeded and sliced
2 cups sugar	
3 eggs	¼ cup shaved citron
1 cup milk	¼ teaspoon each ground cinnamon, cloves, and nutmeg
½ teaspoon vanilla	
½ teaspoon lemon extract	
3 cups flour	1 tablespoon molasses
1 teaspoon cream of tartar and ½ teaspoon soda or	½ teaspoon lemon extract
3 teaspoons baking powder	

The ingredients for the first part of the cake were combined in the usual fashion—flour sifted before measuring, then again with the soda and cream of tartar (or baking powder), butter and sugar well creamed, eggs beaten separately, the whites folded in last. When the batter seemed thoroughly satisfactory as to its lightness and texture, Emily divided it into two parts. One part she baked in two well-buttered and slightly floured square shallow pans in a moderate oven. To the other half of the batter she added the fruit, spices, molasses, and lemon extract, and baked it in two pans like the first part, keeping the oven a little cooler as was right and proper for any batter containing fruit and molasses, as she explained in one of our morning cake-baking sessions. When finished, the four cakes were piled in tiers, first a dark, then a light and so on, with thick layers of bright red jelly between them. Sometimes the cake was iced over its entire surface with a thick white frosting, or some of the bright jelly was whipped into the icing to give it a faint rose tint. Again she might cover it heavily with chocolate frosting studded with halved nut meats. One never knew just how Ribbon Cake would be finished and embellished, which made it all the more fascinating.

Emily adored white cake, and Snow Cake was probably her favorite. She made it less often than some of her other fine cakes, however—possibly because it was a rich cake, and she always liked to keep something in reserve for great occasions. Snow Cake, put together in a unique way, was, when finished, so fleecy white and delicate that it seemed almost too ethereal to eat. Here is the receipt for it as I copied it from her private collection many years ago:

⌦ Snow Cake ⌫

1 cup butter	1 cup cornstarch
2 cups sugar	3 teaspoons baking powder
8 egg whites	⅛ teaspoon almond extract
1 cup milk	¼ teaspoon vanilla extract
1½ cups flour	

The flour for this cake was always sifted many times, "to make it very light," Emily explained. Then she measured it, added the baking powder and cornstarch, and sifted it again, perhaps twice. The butter, never skimpily measured, was beaten until it resembled pale golden whipped cream, and then added to the flour with further vigorous beating. The egg whites were also beaten alone until very stiff; then the sifted sugar was gradually folded into them. To the flour and butter mixture the milk was slowly added. Next the egg whites and sugar, whipped to stiff peaks, and the flavoring were carefully incorporated. The batter looked good enough to eat without baking, but Emily ignored my hints and spooned it into a carefully buttered tube pan and baked it in what she called a "moderate oven." Emily never liked her cakes to become a deep brown; she preferred them a pale biscuit color or a delicate tan. When Snow Cake, covered with a thick white icing, was cut, the slices showed a very distinct but faint brown line between the snowy cake and the snowier icing, which always seemed to make the cake even more attractive.

A celebrated cake in our household was Harlequin Cake. We all loved it, except my father, who always shunned it himself and frequently warned us not to eat it.

"No food was ever intended to be colored like that," he would say splutteringly. "If you eat it and are poisoned, you will have no one to blame but yourselves."

But we never listened to him and no one ever suffered any ill effects no matter how much of the rainbow-tinted cake was eaten.

The foundation was a favorite receipt:

⤜⟫ HARLEQUIN CAKE ⟪⤛

1 cup butter	1 teaspoon vanilla extract
2 cups sugar	6 egg whites
1 cup milk	Pink coloring
3 cups flour	Green coloring
2 squares baking chocolate	Pinch of cinnamon
3 teaspoons baking powder	

The ingredients were put together in Emily's usual

way. When the batter was white and cloud-like it was divided into four parts, one of which was left white; to another enough beet juice to produce a pale pink was added, to the third was added the green juice extracted from spinach, squeezed through a bit of cheesecloth, and the fourth was made rich by the incorporation of two squares of cooking chocolate, melted over hot water, with a pinch, very tiny, of cinnamon blended with it. When the batter was just right as to tints and lightness, it was baked in four layer-cake pans, and put together with a refreshing lemon honey. This filling formed a delicate yellow dividing line between the brown, pink, white and green layers and the effect was very pretty. White frosting coated the entire luscious surface and was sometimes sprinkled with pink sugar or grated chocolate for additional beautification. Harlequin Cake, like most of Emily's best cake receipts, was subject to many variations. Now and then she omitted the green layer and substituted a second white layer or chopped raisins or nuts might be put into the chocolate layer. No matter how she embellished the cake, to us youngsters it was always amazingly good. We would eat our share of it layer by layer, picking off the tempting lemon honey to be devoured all by itself when the noble cake had become a mere memory. Unfortunately, Harlequin Cake was regarded as purely company fare, and then of course it would have been rude to ask for more than two helpings of it, so we never had quite enough of it to satisfy our greedy cravings.

Emily made the lemon honey for her delicious cake by grating the rinds and squeezing the juice from two lemons, adding a generous cup of sugar, an equally generous tablespoon of butter, and the yolks of two or three eggs. After beating all the ingredients together well, the mixture was cooked, with constant stirring in a small saucepan on the back of the stove. When cool it was almost transparent and just thick enough to spread nicely.

Watermelon Cake still brings memories of afternoon tea in the garden with honeysuckle and sweet white petunias wafting their faint perfume toward us as we sat in our frilled and starched lawn dresses, very polite and proper, while Mother entertained distant cousins or old friends on their annual calls. It was a mysterious and fascinating cake and always brought forth exclamations of delight from our guests. Probably that was one reason why Emily liked to make it.

Watermelon Cake was one of those particular cakes that required two persons to put it together successfully. Sometimes I was permitted to assist in the tricky process, and always very proud occasions those were! Snow Cake was the basis for this picturesque cake, as it was for so many of my sister's best and showiest creations, and I think she preferred the Watermelon receipt to all others. The batter, when beautifully smooth and light, was divided into two parts. One half was left plain. Into the other half of the batter, colored a decided pink with the ever faithful beet juice, about one cupful of thoroughly washed and dried currants, powdered with flour, were stirred. When all was ready and an oval cake pan had been buttered and slightly floured, a tube of stiff paper some four inches in diameter and buttered inside and out, was placed in the center of the pan, one of the cake-makers holding it firmly in place, while the other poured the white batter all round it and spooned the currant-dotted pink batter inside. Then the tube was withdrawn, oh, so cautiously, and the cake was carefully placed in the oven to bake slowly to a creamy suntan tint. When finished, cooled for a moment, and turned meticulously from the pan, it was heavily coated all over with icing tinted a naturalistic green with crushed spinach leaves.

Such a to-do from our guests when it was cut, revealing white outer portion, pink, seeded center, and green icing rind! Watermelon Cake was one of Emily's greatest achievements. I can still recollect her look of relieved triumph when the cake proved perfect, for there was always some doubt as to whether the pink section would stay where it belonged or spill itself and its seeds into the white border.

Sunshine Cake was another treasured cake which required the efforts of two persons to bring it to that state of exquisite fluffiness which was the mark of a perfect sponge cake. The receipt, in faded writing on a bit of torn, discolored paper that smelled vaguely of vanilla, read:

"Two persons must make this cake. One beats the whites of the eggs——etc., etc." Therefore Emily and Maud usually forgathered importantly in the kitchen for its manufacture. But because all the ingredients must be weighed instead of measured and because there was some doubt as to the amounts of sugar and flour—the paper being torn just at this important juncture—my sisters were never quite sure about them, and results were not always what they expected.

"Half the weight of the eggs in sugar," one maintained. "Half the weight of the eggs in flour," declared the other.

Finally Aunt Eliza, herself no mean cook, came for a visit and with her assistance and advice, the receipt was reduced to this simple formula:

⮌ SUNSHINE CAKE ⮌

1 cup granulated sugar	5 egg whites
⅔ cup flour	1 teaspoon grated lemon rind
¼ teaspoon cream of tartar	A dash of lemon juice
7 egg yolks	

The original receipt had called for ten eggs and no

leavening whatever, but Aunt Eliza's receipt made a cake just as large and fine, and everyone was satisfied. Besides as she explained, that tiny mite of cream of tartar removed all possibility of doubt as to the cake's lightness, and, because of the fewer eggs, required, we might have it more frequently. So instead of being just a summer cake, Sunshine became a year-round event on our table (unless eggs became an entirely minus quantity). Even our critical father ate it appreciatively, although as a rule he despised butterless cakes. Some of the fun of making it was lost, however, as one person could very well put it together by herself. Besides, I think my sisters rather enjoyed the element of chance which attended the making of the cake by the old torn receipt. When Emily made a Sunshine Cake by Aunt Eliza's method, she beat the egg whites for a few moments, added the cream of tartar, lemon peel and juice, and continued beating them until they stood in peaks, then she whipped the sugar in lightly. The yolks of the eggs were beaten to a creamy froth, then added to the whites and sugar, and the flour, sifted three times, folded in gently. Three quarters of an hour in a moderate oven served to bake Sunshine Cake perfectly.

Currant Cake was one of my sister's own inventions—a layer cake, so to speak, but we never regarded it in any other way than merely "Emily's Currant Cake"—in modern vernacular, a whale of a cake. Father ate it without comment, which meant that he thoroughly approved of and enjoyed it; we younger children made little gluttons of ourselves whenever we had a chance; and Uncle George, who was something of a gourmet, pronounced it excellent and always managed to get the very last piece for himself. This fine-textured, buttercup-yellow cake Emily made after this receipt:

⌒ CURRANT CAKE ⌒

¾ cup butter	3 cups flour
2 cups sugar	3 teaspoons baking powder
4 egg yolks	Grated rind of half an
2 egg whites	orange or lemon
1 cup milk	

The currants were used in the icing only, which was the novel touch. Emily combined the ingredients for the cake by her usual method, adding the stiffly beaten egg whites last. She baked it in two shallow rectangular pans—round ones would do as well, I suppose, but to me the cake would lose half its old charm if the shape were changed. The filling was the original part and gave the cake its name. Emily beat the two remaining egg whites to a stiff foam, adding a pinch of cream of tartar and half an egg-shell of cold water, then she sifted in fine powdered sugar until the icing was just stiff enough to spread, when the juice of half an orange or lemon was whipped in and the beating continued. When the icing had become fleecy white and puffy, she stirred in half a pound of well-washed and dried currants, first plumping them a bit in the oven, with more sugar if necessary. This filling was spread half an inch thick between the layers, a little more conservatively over the top.

Fig Cake was a classic in our household. I never learned its origin but no words of mine can describe its lusciousness. I think it was the most delectable of all my sister's cakes, but she reserved it for rare and unusual occurrences, one of which stands out conspicuously in my memory.

Fig Cake was her *pièce de résistance* for the New Year's refreshment table. There it stood surrounded by every known variety of cakes, large and small, by sandwiches and salads, but it dwarfed them all with its heavily iced and gleaming magnificence. When cut in generous squares it disclosed a thick yellow layer enriched with delicately sliced figs and enveloped in two silvery white layers, a mouth-watering icing oozing alluringly between. It was a mysterious sort of cake, and one that might seem rather intricate, but Emily did it all so easily, spreading the icing so deftly in great ridges between the layers and over the whole surface of the wonderful cake, that it appeared one of the easiest things in the world.

New Year's Day was an exciting, thrilling day, especially for my sisters, for it was the one occasion in the whole year when *young men* might come to our home openly and fearlessly, and they made the most of it.

Father thoroughly approved the custom. Indeed, he went calling himself, beginning his rounds quite early in the day and returning home in time for the substantial tea which concluded the day's festivities. The morning was a busy one for us all, and seemed especially so for me, but I enjoyed it all. No end of demands upon me could possibly damp my enthusiasm or quench my energy. First I must bring hot water for Father's shaving, then dash from room to room where my sisters and the young ladies who were to receive with them were dressing, with pins, curling irons, powder boxes, combs, and what not. Then back I must run, to smooth Father's silk hat with a piece of worn velvet, on to the dining room where Mother and Aunt Sophie were putting the finishing touches to the table, and out to the carriage house to hurry Emil, who was giving a last dusting to the carriage, which was only taken out from under its stout dust sheets on state occasions like this. Usually the old Democrat wagon was quite good enough for Father, but on New Year's Day he sat in solitary grandeur on the back seat while Emil, gotten up in fine style, drove him about to Mrs. Harding's, Lizzie Dexter's, the Hodges' and other old friends' homes to pay his respects.

Anna, in a bright blue silk dress, and wearing gold earrings, would open the front door to admit the gentlemen who came calling at our house. It was all arranged beautifully.

At last everything was ready; often, however, not until the first caller made his appearance, much to our consternation, even though it might be only Sam Parkes or Willie McAlister, whom my sisters had known since fourth-reader days. But today was different; everything was very grand and formal. The parlors were darkened, of course, and the chandeliers lighted. An elegant silver card receiver was placed conspicuously on the marble table in the hall, and a huge bouquet of lifelike, clove-scented paper carnations, over which my sisters had toiled many a night when they should have been sleeping, reposed on the center table in the front parlor.

My sisters were grandly dressed for this grand occasion in sequin-trimmed silks, the overskirts bordered with rows and rows of fringed knife pleating. Emily and Maud wore gold watches, fastened with large gold pins over their hearts, the long gold watch chains draped about their necks. Molly was considered too young for such display, but for festive occasions like this Aunt Sophie could always be counted upon to lend her cameo bracelet. Gold bracelets encircled the arms of the older girls, and all three wore high buttoned shoes. I thought I had never seen them look so beautiful.

It was a great time and New Year's calling a great institution. Upstairs in the large sewing room over the parlor, Kitty and I discreetly watched the callers come and go, sometimes singly, sometimes by twos and threes. Now and then a group of daring young men would arrive in a hack—and that was very exciting, something to be talked about for months. Even Mother and Aunt Sophie had callers—Mr. Peacock, Mr. Scales Dr. Miller, perhaps the minister, and each and all were escorted to the dining room for sandwiches, coffee, and cake. The table was filled with good things from which to make a selection.

Uncle George was the only one who seemed to be left out of all the gaiety, but poor Uncle George cared little for social affairs; he was a literary man and thought us all very silly, so he remained in his room and wrote sonnets, appearing only when, at seven o'clock, the stress of the entertaining had abated and Father, having dutifully called on all the ladies on his list, would return in high good humor for his tea.

Perhaps a few friends might have been invited also, and I can even recall occasions when one or two of my sisters' beaux were asked to remain. New Year's tea was always set forth on our old walnut table, polished every morning by Emil with a brick sewn in many thicknesses of old blanket. I remember how it mirrored the silver cake basket and the tea service. We waited on ourselves on New Year's evening so that Anna and Emil might go to a party of their own on Clybourne Avenue. There were always sandwiches, plenty of them, for Anna was a master hand at their manufacture, but the chief glories of the table were the cakes on their silver plates and high glass stand. There were many varieties, but Fig Cake seemed to me the most beautiful and delightful of them all.

Fig Cake was made in two parts, each delicate but rich. When finished it was at least six inches high with its gleaming icing and filling. Emily baked it in long shallow pans.

∽ FIG CAKE ∾

Silver Part

½ cup butter	2 cups flour
1½ cups sugar	2 teaspoons baking powder
¾ cup milk	½ teaspoon vanilla
5 egg whites	

The batter was prepared by the usual method, adding the stiffly beaten egg whites last. Emily very carefully baked the cake in two long shallow pans.

Gold Part

½ cup butter
1 cup sugar
½ cup milk
½ teaspoon lemon extract
pinch of cinnamon
1½ cups flour

1½ teaspoons baking
   powder
7 egg yolks
1 whole egg
1 pound of figs

The egg yolks and the whole egg were beaten until very light and foamy, flour sifted, measured, and sifted again with the baking powder and cinnamon. Then the ingredients were combined in the usual way. Half the batter was smoothly arranged in a long shallow pan and covered with a layer of figs which had been washed, well dried, thinly sliced, and slightly floured. The rest of the batter was spooned over them and the cake baked in a moderate oven. When nicely done, not too brown, it was turned from the pan and placed between two layers of silver cake, with a thick rich white icing flavored with lemon or almond between. The whole cake, top and sides, was covered lusciously with the same icing, and this masterpiece added the crowning touch to our New Year's happiness.

Maud Conquers Kisses

*I*T WAS MAUD who introduced Devil's Food into our midst. Maud was sociably inclined, made friends readily, and was constantly enlarging her circle. She loved visiting, for the afternoon, for supper, or for the night, and never returned to the family fold from these excursions without a bundle of news. It was Maud who kept us abreast of the neighborhood affairs—who had a new baby; who had turned the parlor carpet; who was engaged to be married, and to whom; how many children were in the family just moving into Mrs. Smith's old house; how many jars of strawberry preserves Mrs. Scales had made; the strange but stylish new coat Adelaide Buckingham was wearing. She also gave us colorful descriptions of the newest fashions in hats, and so on and so on. It was quite wonderful to listen to her as she took off her hat and smoothed her bright hair around her fingers, gazing at herself approvingly in the sewing-room looking glass.

Aunt Sophie used to fear Maud was vain, but then she had the only naturally curly hair in the family, hair that Mother twined about a curling stick every morning while Emily vigorously brushed the straight locks on the heads of the rest of us, plaited them in long braids, and tied them with brown "lutestring" ribbon which Father bought by the bolt. Surely with such hair, Maud's vanity was excusable, so we forgave her and listened, fascinated, to the breathless accounts of her visits.

"The Watermans had the most marvelous cake, all chocolate clear through not just the frosting—that was white and thick and tasted a little as though it was flavored with lemon juice. They called it Devil's Food. It was a layer cake put together with white icing, very thick and so delicious. Clara Waterman let me copy the receipt, and I'm going to try it the very first chance I have."

"Clara Waterman?" queried Aunt Sophie, who was slightly deaf and did not always catch names correctly. "Wasn't it one of the Watermans who taught you how to make Angel Cake?" We were rather sorry to have Aunt Sophie ask that question when Maud was so full of news, for Angel Cake had not met with a very cordial reception from Father a few months before, and the subject was still an embarrassing one for Maud.

She had discovered the cake on one of her visits, coaxed Clara for the receipt, and blithely made the cake. I remember how beautiful it looked, so snowy white and airy as she set it proudly on the Sunday evening tea table, and I remember Father's face, too, as he sank his teeth in the fragile morsel. "Paper towels!" was all he said, but it was enough to bring tears of disappointment and mortification to Maud. Of course Father apologized later, after his own fashion, and told Maud her cake was not bad at all—besides, he had meant sheet wadding, not paper towels. However, that was now long past and forgotten and she was happily on the trail of another brand-new cake that sounded very promising and alluring.

"Devil's Food," she continued, not replying to Aunt Sophie's question, "looks lovely in a cake basket with Angel Cake; first a slice of the chocolate, then one of the white, the way the Watermans had it last night. I can

34

scarcely wait to make it."

Her opportunity came soon, for the very next Saturday Mother asked Emily to drive her into the city on a shopping tour, and Maud was left in full possession of the kitchen, with Anna to help her.

I asked for the job but was refused, as the new cake demanded the utmost attention. "But you can watch, and perhaps I may need you, too," my sister said kindly. Watching Maud make a cake was not as educational as helping Emily, but it was far more exciting, for Maud's bent was toward novel, tricky things—cream puffs, kisses, rolled jelly cake (which sometimes refused to roll), and rich cookies that would occasionally stick to the board, no matter how tenderly Maud treated them.

Delicious things, every one, we younger children thought, because now and then, for some reason or other—perhaps because of too generous measuring or too little baking—Maud's masterpieces developed a chewy, candylike quality that made them different and delightful. Unfortunately, from our point of view, this did not happen often, and when it did, Maud never said much about the matter, but Kitty and I usually had a picnic with the tempting, chewy cakes as our *pièce de résistance*. They did not last long, particularly if our bosom friend, Millie Andress, was our guest. Millie's family baked cakes, too, but theirs were rather plain cakes and were made only to commemorate some such important event as the anniversary of the Great Fire, or the day Mr. Andress had sung in the church choir, so Millie approved Maud's cookery misfortunes quite as warmly as we did and only regretted that they were not of more frequent occurrence.

Devil's Food, though a new cake in our household, had made its dashing appearance in Chicago in the middle eighties, and by the time it reached our quiet little community, was quite the rage. Maud's receipt was the original one, and made a large, dark, rich cake. Here it is:

⟡ DEVIL'S FOOD ⟡

½ cup butter
2 cups sugar
5 eggs
1 cup sour cream
2½ cups flour

1 scant teaspoon soda
1 teaspoon baking powder
3 squares unsweetened
    chocolate
1 teaspoon vanilla

Anna melted the chocolate over hot water while Maud creamed the butter and added the sugar gradually; then she whipped in the slightly beaten yolks of the eggs and the melted chocolate and vanilla. I was permitted to sift and measure the flour and then sift it again with the baking powder and soda. When this was done, Maud alternately added the flour mixture and the sour cream to the egg-sugar-butter-chocolate combination. Last of all, she folded in the stiffly beaten whites of the eggs and turned the delicious-smelling brown batter into three layer-cake pans which Anna had buttered and floured. The baking, in a very moderate oven, was carefully watched. According to a time-honored custom in our family, the cakes were tested with a clean broomstraw and when finished were turned, beautifully brown and entrancingly fragrant, from the pans onto a clean towel.

Now came the next important part, the icing and filling. The Watermans' receipt called for a thick boiled icing made pleasantly piquant with a few drops of citric acid. But citric acid sounded dangerous to Maud, and besides, as Anna explained, we had no such article in our supply closet. Even Emily's stock of special flavorings refused to yield it, so Maud used lemon juice, sparingly and judiciously, and the result was perfect.

Altogether it was a noble cake, nobly made. Maud was scarlet of face, her curls in tight ringlets all round her temples and neck, and she had several splotches of chocolate on her white apron, but the cake looked, as it tasted, superb, and even Father approved of it. Secretly, I have always thought its name appealed to him.

So Devil's Food came to our household and was duly included in our list of cakes we could not do without. It was truly a delectable cake, darker and more moist than the modern chocolate cake, its icing always thick and white, sometimes flavored with orange juice, again with vanilla or lemon, and once with almond. It had good keeping qualities, too, Mother used to say, if a trusty hiding place could be found for it. The old crock was just no good at all.

Jelly Kisses came to us through another source, but it was Maud who first attempted them, and Maud who finally achieved cake fame almost equal to Emily's through her success with the delicate bits of confectionery.

Vivacious, redheaded, brown-eyed Ida Savage brought Jelly Kisses as her contribution to a Sunday School feast. They were mysterious morsels, all crumbly, sugary, and crunchy on the outside, with a spot of bright red or pale amber jelly hidden within. Even the Sunday School superintendent's wife wanted to know how to make Jelly Kisses, but Ida's big sister May was a little chary with the receipt; so for a long time the Kisses continued to ravish and tantalize us.

"I don't want to seem selfish," May explained wistfully. "But Jelly Kisses are the one thing I can make well, the one thing that makes me popular, and if everyone else makes them I won't have any charm at all."

But when Maud promised to teach her to make Devil's Food, May succumbed, for Devil's Food, since Maud's discovery, had become quite celebrated in our circle.

Maud had tried every receipt for kisses she could find, but in some way or another had always met with failure.

Usually the delicate little cakes had risen like balloons in the oven, and her spirits had risen with them, only to fall as the cakes fell into flat, sticky, pancakelike affairs, so unattractive as almost to drive her to tears.

"Such kisses!" she would exclaim, as she scraped the sugary remnants into my eager keeping.

But being a stubborn young woman, she refused to yield to so small a thing as a Jelly Kiss. So she added various ingredients to the receipt—flour, cornstarch, baking powder, more sugar, another egg white, but all to no purpose. Now May had promised to teach her the right method, and she was jubilant.

May's receipt was a distinct disappointment, however, for it was so like all the others she had tried; but May went calmly ahead with her egg beating and sugar sifting and instructions. The receipt read:

⟨⟩ JELLY KISSES ⟨⟩

3 egg whites
1 scant cup fine granulated
    sugar

½ teaspoon vanilla or other
    extract

"The main thing is to have the eggs cold and to take care that no speck of yolk gets into the whites when you break them. Then beat them until you can turn the bowl upside down without spilling a particle," directed May. "See, they are just right now." And, suiting the action to the word, she proceeded: "Add half the sugar and beat again very hard, beat and beat until the egg whites and sugar stand in peaks, then stir in the rest of the sugar and the flavoring without much beating—that's all."

May had brought over her baking board, a small plank of oak to be used instead of a pan, but later Maud found that any heavy dripping pan would answer if she inverted it and wet it thoroughly with cold water, as May had done with the board. The surface of the board was covered with a sheet of white paper, also moistened on the underside. Then the fluffy, airy mixture was dropped from the tip of a tablespoon, which May dipped in hot water, in neat little mounds on the paper, not more than an inch and a half apart.

"Of course you don't expect them to flatten down and run all together," remarked Maud, "or you wouldn't put them so close together."

"No, they won't behave like that," May replied, "for we beat them too hard. They're going to be all right—just wait!"

Baking the kisses was equally as important as beating them, it seemed. The oven must be barely warm. "They should really only dry out," said May. "Too much heat will make them rise up and burst, or if they don't burst they'll flatten and run together. Keep the oven cool and let the kisses have a full hour to bake. They won't be too brown—you'll see."

And true enough, they acted exactly as May had foretold: they came from the oven a pale, creamy tan and light as air. May showed Maud how to make a little opening in the bottom of each one, scrape out a bit of the soft center and slip in a spoonful of jelly.

And wasn't Maud proud when she produced her first batch of Jelly Kisses all by herself? And how earnestly she worked, beating and beating the egg whites testing the heat of the oven a dozen times with a bit of white paper, and scarcely daring to walk across the kitchen once the precious things had been given to the keeping of the old stove, for fear of jiggling them.

And now both young women had two claims to fame, where each had had but one before, for Maud kept her promise to May, and Devil's Food was as proudly set forth on the Savage table as were the kisses on our own.

Of course Maud had to try a few tricks with the kisses as soon as she mastered the technique of their making. Sometimes she added a tablespoon of cocoa to the egg white and sugar mixture, or perhaps she would fold in half a cup of chopped nut meats. That was an incomparable touch! Anna and I (nothing could keep me away from the kitchen on one of Maud's mornings there) shared the little scooped-out bits between us, for Anna was a perpetual child in many ways—one of them was her fondness for licking bowls and scraping pans.

My sisters never encroached on each other's territory. Jelly Kisses were Maud's exclusive property just as Harlequin Cake was Emily's. Assist each other they would willingly, and frequently did, but I have often wondered what might have happened to Jelly Kisses if Emily, with her imagination and her daring, had not been quite so conscientious. Wonderful things, I'll wager!

Cream Puffs were Maud's own especial pet project, too, and she made them well. In fact I believe no confectioner's shop, either in the eighties or since, could have improved on the light, delicate, crispy puffs she used to turn out for the family on those occasions when something extra special was demanded. But she learned by experience and by many sad tragedies.

How many disappointing cream puffs I ate to help Maud get them out of the way, I could never have counted. Fortunately eggs and butter were never costly purchases in those days, so a few failures more or less did not matter—that is, not very much.

Maud just could not believe a receipt; she had to add, subtract, multiply, or divide it many times before she would admit that perhaps it was all right just as it stood. So it was with Cream Puffs. One book said: "1 cup of hot water, ½ cup of butter, 1 cup of flour, and 3 large or 4 small eggs."

"Why water," asked Maud, "when we have so much milk and everyone knows milk is more nourishing than water? And no baking powder!—how do they ever expect the puffs to puff?"

So, on her first experiment she substituted milk for water and added baking powder. When they were finished the puffs resembled fairly good muffins. We all ate them without complaint, but could not forbear voicing our disappointment, even though Maud poured the filling "English cream," the book called it—over them.

"There was no other place for it," she wailed. But soon she tried again, adding more and then more baking powder, with the result that we had muffins again and again, lighter than the first, and drier, really not as good, but still eatable.

Everyone offered suggestions. "Why not try something easier?" asked Mother. "More eggs," counseled Aunt Sophie. "Hotter stove," was Anna's advice. But Emil, coming with the milk pails early one morning when Maud, who, as I have intimated, was a rather determined young woman, was preparing once more to attack cream puffs, solved the problem. "Miss Maudie, you have mooch patience," he remarked, glancing at her worried face. "But I tink you made big mistake you don't do so as the book say. I going to make big mistakes many times when I do not do what Big Boss say. Maybe book is your big boss."

"Perhaps there is something in that after all," said Maud. "Although I still think the receipt is wrong, but I'll try it just for once, anyway, then I'm through."

And strange to say, the book was right, although it was a very old bakers' manual, and the quantities called for were huge and the directions slightly vague. But Maud subtracted and divided until she had a family-sized formula, and went to work. "Chou Paste" was the official name for the cream-puff batter, and the receipt as Maud finally worked it out went this way:

❧ CREAM PUFFS ❧

1 cup boiling water	4 eggs
½ cup butter	1 teaspoon grated lemon rind
1 tablespoon sugar	½ teaspoon salt
1 cup flour	

"Put the water into a scrupulously clean saucepan with the sugar, salt, lemon rind, and butter. When it boils turbulently, add all the flour, stirring diligently until the mixture leaves the sides of the saucepan; then cook more mildly, but continue to stir for as long as it takes you to count twenty. Remove from the fire and leave to cool, with occasional stirring. When this is accomplished, beat in the eggs one by one, make into small balls the size of walnuts, for the cakes will grow to a great size in the baking, and put on an oiled baking sheet. Bake in flash heat or in moderate oven."

The receipt was followed faithfully, although Maud was so impatient to get her puffs into the oven she could scarcely wait for the paste to cool before adding the eggs. That process, too, was very discouraging. The first egg just would not allow itself to be mixed with the paste, which on its part seemed to resent the intrusion and broke into little unmanageable bits. Then just as Maud about decided that the whole thing was a failure and was contemplating throwing it to the hens, it suddenly became smooth and pliant and velvety. The next egg was added confidently, and the whole thing was to be done over again, but finally all the eggs were beaten in and the batter was deeply golden, smooth and actually looked as though it might be right.

Baking was a puzzle, for Maud had not the least idea what "flash heat" might mean, but moderate oven was a familiar term, so the puffs, made into small balls, were baked about forty minutes. And they puffed and puffed, really in a charming way; some of them, because of impatience in taking them from the oven a little too soon, sagged a bit, but even those could be filled with the English Cream and they tasted quite as good as the others which were more substantially baked.

English Cream was so nice that later we found many uses for it other than filling cream puffs. It was made by first steeping two or three bits of thin lemon rind in a pint of milk on the back of the stove, then heating it to boiling and adding ¼ cup sugar beaten with two eggs, a tablespoon of flour, and a speck of salt. Cooked slowly to prevent curdling, the cream became a delicate, slightly thickened sauce, which when cool was just right for filling the puffs. The bakers' manual directed that it be poured rapidly from one jug to another until sufficiently cold and well mixed, which seemed a little complex to us, but Maud followed the advice obediently and ardently. When the puffs were cool she made little slits in the sides and spooned the cooled filling in delicately, her eyes shining and her hands trembling. Then she sprinkled them all with powdered sugar and set them forth on Mother's best silver plate.

We had only a few of those first successful Cream Puffs for our supper that night, for Maud went calling on the Watermans and took with her the lovely silver plate filled with the delectable puffs all covered with a fine napkin, but before she left Emil was rewarded with one of the very best and most beautiful Cream Puffs of them all.

Gaufres, another cake described in the old manual, intrigued Maud's fancy next and Gaufres she must make, although Mother tried to persuade her that with Jelly

Kisses and Cream Puffs she had established herself as a successful cakemaker. But I think Maud must have dreamed Gaufres, for she was constantly harping on them.

"They would look so pretty with the Jelly Kisses when you have company for tea," she would say, "and besides, I'm almost sure they are easy to make. After all, they sound as though they were simply rolled cookies."

Of course she got her way, for privately I think Mother was curious about them herself, so Maud made them, and except for a few perfectly sumptuous ones that would not roll and therefore fell into my greedy keeping, they were not half the problem that her other two ventures had been.

To be sure Gaufres proper called for some special type of iron that might have been a waffle iron, but then again it might not, and anyway, Maud proposed to make her Gaufres after a method which the manual called "an easy way." So she blended together to a fluffy cream ¼ cup of butter and ½ cup of sifted powdered sugar and just a suspicion of almond extract. Then drop by drop she added ¼ cup of milk alternately with a little less than a cup of flour, about ⅞ of a cup I think she finally decided would be just right.

The mixture was much thicker than a batter, but not as thick as a dough. Next, as she had no cooky sheet such as the manual recommended, she greased the underside of a shallow dripping pan and spread the mixture so very thinly over it that it was barely more than a film, using Father's carving knife for the process; Anna, Emil, who now considered himself an authority on cakemaking, and my officious young self were the audience. The next thing was to mark the film into three-inch squares; for this the back of the knife was brought into action. "A slow oven," directed the book, and a slow oven Anna had ready. The cakes baked in a short time, and came forth an exquisite brown. Now—to roll them. This had to be done very quickly and while they were still warm and pliable, so Maud set the pan on the back of the stove, separated the cakes deftly and then, with a dull knife and her fingers, rolled them up neatly. Success on the first venture! No wonder she was happy and excited—and Mother proudly served Gaufres that very afternoon when some of her friends dropped in for a rubber of whist and a cup of tea.

The subject of icings and like embellishments was for long a ticklish one in our household of good cakes and cakemakers. Mother was of the opinion that a cake, if it was honestly good and well made, needed no trimmings whatever; to add them, she declared, was like gilding the lily. Now and then, to be sure, a little fine sugar might be sifted over the top, or one might even go as far as glazing a special cake with a paste made of fine powdered sugar and sweet cream; but as for elaborate finishes and toppings, they were unnecessary and extravagant. To all of which Aunt Sophie nodded approval, adding that she preferred brown sugar and slightly soured cream to Mother's idea of the paste finish.

Emily, whose cakes were usually crested with a rich, smooth icing, argued that a fine cake was made even more distinguished by a fine icing. Her preference was for the uncooked variety, the kind she made for her Currant Cake; merely egg white, a little cold water, fine sugar, much beating, and, as an aristocratic touch, a few drops, only a very few, mind, of some fragrant, delicate extract.

"And that's all there is to it," she would remark as she smoothed the knife over a perfect cake, perfectly iced. "No trouble, no worry, no failures."

Maud, who, as I have remarked, went visiting around far more than anyone else in the family and brought home more ideas than she had any possible use for, was all for glistening boiled icings. The Watermans, who at one time, represented for her the maximum of perfection in every-thing from cakemaking to amateur theatricals, always made boiled icings, and no one could deny their cakes were glorious; so Maud continued to make boiled icings, which, I fear, to Emily's secret satisfaction, did not always prove quite as glorious as Maud would have wished.

One winter when surprise parties were very much the vogue, Sadie Lindley, a popular young lady in my sisters' clique, was selected as the victim, and of course cakes were much in demand; every girl promised to bring one of her own making.

Maud compromised on Gaufres, as they were her lat-est achievement; Emily made her Snow Cake and smoth-ered it in heavy white icing faintly flavored with almond and garnished with blanched almonds cut in long slivers. Molly, with Mother's assistance, struggled over a simple Orange Sponge Cake, finished merely with a sifting of powdered sugar. Clara Waterman's contribution was a handsome Devil's Food swathed in heavy boiled icing, the filling enriched with finely chopped hickory-nut meats. It was a luscious cake, as I could testify, for Maud brought me a bit which I ate for my breakfast the next morning.

The cakes were all prize winners, everyone declared, just as though it had been a contest instead of a surprise party. Old Grandpa Lindley swore he had not tasted such an Orange Sponge Cake since his mother died; it was exactly the kind he liked, so Molly was happy.

Clara Waterman had confided to Sadie she had been terribly afraid beforehand that Emily's cake was going to taste eggy with all that raw icing on it, but that it had not at all; in fact, she thought it wonderful, and intended ask-ing Emily to show her how to make it. And Emily, in talk-ing over the party with Mother, said she had been all in a tremble when Clara's cake was cut, for she expected the icing to crumble and fall the minute the knife touched it;

46

but that it had done nothing of the kind, and was beautiful and very delicious.

Whereupon my family came to a weighty conclusion. Some cakes, like Mother's delicate Sponge, were better after all with no trimmings at all except the simple powdering with fine sugar, or with a very modest icing of sugar blended with cream or fruit juice, spread very thinly over the cake. For large, imposing cakes, the icing might be cooked or not, as one preferred, if it were properly made; and for those elaborate affairs like Devil's Food, where the icing would also act as filling, the boiled variety, though more tricky, was probably the best.

This important matter having been settled and our conclusions painstakingly set down in my sisters' personal cookery diaries, we went on our cake-making ways content.

Mother's Five-Foot Bookshelf

ALF-HIDDEN in a little nook under the stairway in our hall was a shelf filled with musty old books, most of them Mother's, and all of them too shabby to be permitted in the parlor, but I loved them every one.

There was *Fern Leaves*, by a lady who called herself Fanny Fern. Fanny wrote very touchingly about simple, everyday things that might happen anywhere. "Rainy Days," "Bluestocking Ladies," "Funerals," and so on—no topic was too insignificant or too melancholy for her pen. Several novels, such as *Pink and White Tyranny*—which was regarded as a very daring piece of writing—*The Minister's Wooing*, and *Jane Eyre*, likewise had their places on the shelf. Then there was a volume of collected verse which Uncle George commended highly to my sisters, and two beautiful but ornate books, bound in fragrant Russia leather, gold illumined, and further embellished with steel engravings and watercolor illustrations. *Leaflets of Memory* was the title of one, and the other was *The Language of Flowers*, or, *The Pilgrimage of Love*.

A large, brown, very disheveled book, consulted frequently and considered a family treasure, was Chambers' *Information for the People*. Between its broken and discolored covers it contained the most wonderful assortment of knowledge ever assembled in so small a space, I imagine. This volume was my helpful and responsive friend when a composition had to be written, and gave its valuable aid to Uncle George when he was in sore need of a tuneful or a witty word to finish his daily poem. Father depended wholly on its sage advice if a horse or cow or hen were ailing. Indeed, he very often declared that without Chambers' *Information* he could never have brought his two prized mares through the terrible scourge of epizooty in 1871. I very much think too, that he relied largely on Mr. Chambers whenever a member of his family was taken ill, for it was on the rarest of occasions that a physician was called upon to prescribe for us. Mr. Chambers did all that adequately.

But of all the cherished books in Mother's out-at-the-elbows collection, I loved best those dealing with foods and cookery. My pet volume was a threadbare affair which had lost its covers and could not be identified. The flyleaves, however, though yellowed and spotted, were intact, and here in faded writing one could read the saga of the book. In 1828 it had been bestowed upon "Charlotte Stayton by her devoted mother," who unfortunately failed to sign her name. Charlotte Stayton in turn had bequeathed it to her beloved daughter, and finally it found its way to my own mother, with her mother's blessing and the admonition never to forget that the way to a man's heart is through his stomach. And I am sure no one who knew her could ever accuse Mother of ignoring her parent's good counsel.

On these pages expressive notations, still fairly legible, amounting almost to a diary or log had also been set down by the different owners of the book in penmanship of such dissimilarity and in inks so varied and faded as to add much charm and mystery to the memoirs. I think one of the most enchanting features the old cookery book offered was the outline of a fat baby hand on one page, all to itself. Mother could tell me nothing about this adorable little hand, except that it had been there as long as she could remember, but under the tracing I used to think I could decipher the words "Little William's Hand," or was it "Little Lillian's Hand"? I could never decide.

My chief diversion in the dusk of a stormy Sunday afternoon, when the memory of the huge dinner I had eaten at one o'clock had somewhat dimmed, was to ensconce myself in a secluded corner of the back parlor and pore over the queerly spelled pages of this cherished book, gloating over its "spunge cakes," "pyes," and "flummeries." I know I must fairly have drooled at some of the descriptions.

Other cookery books Mother owned, of course, more modern ones—Miss Beecher's *Domestic Receipt Book, Modern Cookery in All Its Branches*, by Eliza Acton, "the whole carefully revised by Mrs. S. J. Hale," who was none other than the Mrs. Hale of Godey fame. Another was *The Economical Cook and Housebook*, which, in addition to its rather incomplete receipts, included hints on gardening, and directions for making shoes, for netting a "Very Elegant Tidy," and for constructing a "Practical Ice Chest." There was Miss Leslie's *Receipt Book*, of much later date, which Aunt Sophie considered sinfully extravagant. Mrs. Mary J. Lincoln's was still another, I believe; some time later *Ten Dollars Enough*, a very modern and exciting book by Catherine Owen, was added.

But Mother really had little need of cookbooks, for from those very women who had once owned the queer old volumes she had inherited not only a penchant for cookery, but such a store of priceless receipts and such a wealth of cookery lore that to her family she seemed as well equipped to prepare a dinner for Queen Victoria as to make a simple cake for her children.

Everything Mother made was good. Her meats, roasted to a crispy perfection as to exterior, were rare but never too rare within; and as for her gravies—words fail me. Pastry, as she made it, was of the kind that must have been Henry Ward Beecher's inspiration when he wrote his memorable essay on Apple Pie, but Mother's apple pies, I think, would have proved a still greater lure. They were of the deep-dish variety, with an inverted cup in the center to imprison some of the rich, clove-scented juices. A pastry rose, the making of which was a fascinating thing to watch, ornamented the very center of the flaky crust. But it was her bread and rolls and yeast-risen cakes which set her apart from all the other good cooks in our family, and it is of one of those old-time yeast-risen cakes that I always think when I hear discussions of old-time cakes.

The receipt, to my great joy, was supplied by the queer old book without covers. We called this cake of our delight Bread Cake, because for its foundation it required the same dough that Mother set for our Saturday loaves. Certain down-East friends, however, used to tell us that its correct name was Election Day Cake, and that it was closely associated with the early history of America. But Mother, backed by Uncle George and Aunt Sophie, insisted that it was merely a modification of an old English cake, popular in the mother country for centuries. Be that as it may, Mother made her Bread Cake after the receipt in the old book, and very delicious it was, no matter what its origin. The receipt read something like this:

"Take a quartern of bread dough light for the pans, put to it one half pound sweet butter, one quarter pound beaten and sifted sugar, one half pound raisins of the sun, one half pound Zante currants, candied peel if you please, four new laid eggs, such spices as you favor, and flour as much as you may need." The butter and sugar were creamed together and worked into the dough "light for the pans"; and by the way, a quartern meant to my mother as much as would comfortably fill our old cracked coffee cup, pressed down and running over. I think she lessened the quantity of butter slightly, too, and as for the sugar, there was no possible necessity for beating and sifting the good granulated sort Father always purchased by the barrel. Mother explained that in her childhood sugar was bought by the loaf, great mounds of it, weighing from twenty to forty pounds, which had to be crushed and sifted before even a teaspoonful could be used. We sighed in regret and rapture; regret for the good old days, and rapture that such beating and pounding as she described would never fall to our lot.

Well, as I was saying, the butter and sugar, having been creamed, were worked into the dough, also the well-beaten eggs, and the spices, about one-half teaspoon each of cinnamon, nutmeg, and mace. More sifted flour was gradually stirred into the batter alternately with the raisins and currants, and of combined citron, orange, and lemon peel thinly shaved, about one cup. When the batter was very stiff, entirely too stiff for further beating it was turned in to a well-greased and slightly floured loaf-cake or tube pan and set to rise for an hour, or longer if necessary. When it was light and bubbly it was given to the old oven's care for anywhere from one to one and a half hours, the oven being what Mother called "steady but not too hot." It was a handsome loaf when it was turned from the pan on a clean cloth and left on the table to cool. Even Father, when he dropped into the kitchen for his afternoon hunger appeaser, respected it and left its fragrant, nut-brown crust intact.

Sweet Rusks were regarded as cakes in our family, they were so light and tender and delicious, and went so well with Sunday night tea when two or three or even half

VICTORIAN CAKES

a dozen old friends might come calling. Mother usually prepared for these unexpected guests on Saturday, and a pan of her tempting Sweet Rusks was usually hidden away for just such emergencies.

The foundation for the rusks was always the same, though the finished product might be embellished and varied in any number of ways. To one and a half cups of scalded milk, two tablespoons of butter, four of sugar, and a teaspoon of salt were added, then cooled to lukewarm. Meantime one cake of compressed yeast was crumbled in one half cup of tepid water, sprinkled with half a teaspoon of sugar, and left in a sheltered place to become frothy and light. While all this was going on, one of us would sift from four to five cups of flour, and Mother would begin adding it very gradually to the milk, beating it in well, and when she had a nice, thick, smooth batter, in would go the yeast, with more beating. Two or three eggs, depending on the season and the price, would also be whipped in, and more flour would be incorporated slowly, until the dough could be kneaded. This was a delicate job, as Mother believed in keeping it as soft as possible. But by dipping her fingers in soft butter and working carefully, she managed to work it to a springy, vibrant mass with very little additional flour. She then put it in a clean bowl, covered it with a cloth, and left it in a sheltered nook to expand. In two hours or less it would have doubled its size, seeming to be almost alive with its bursting air bubbles. But it was not ready for the pans yet, by any means. Mother would break all the bubbles with the tips of her fingers and push the dough down until it was just a small ball. Then it would be turned over, the top brushed with soft butter, and left to try its luck again. And again Mother would doom it to disappointment, but finally, after poking it down perhaps three or four times, she would mold it. That was a delicate operation! With the tips of her fingers

54

buttered lightly, she would break off bits of the golden, sweet-smelling dough and roll them quickly and deftly, with as little handling as possible, into balls the size of walnuts. These balls were arranged close together in the buttered baking pans and set aside for the final rising. When they were light as thistledown, they were put in a hot oven and baked about twelve minutes. I can't describe to you the wonderful, ambrosial fragrance that would steal through the house as the rusks came to perfection in the oven. Talk about perfumes of Araby—they could not have compared with Mother's fresh-baked rusks!

But they were not quite finished yet. For added deliciousness Mother glazed them with a blended paste of sugar and cream in equal parts, which she applied with a soft brush; then the rusks went back into the oven for a few moments to dry and take on a most delectable gloss.

One pan of these tempting morsels we sometimes had for our Sunday morning breakfast, and how good they were with coffee or milk! Sometimes we ate them cold; again they were wrapped in brown paper and heated quickly in the oven. Sometimes they were torn apart, never cut, and toasted on the top grate of the oven. No matter how they were served they were the best Sweet Rusks in the world, in our opinion. For tea, they were also reheated, or toasted, and served with raspberry and currant jam or quince honey, and always, whenever she served them to her visitors, Mother had to write the receipt for them to carry home.

The same receipt, embellished slightly, she used for Hot Cross Buns, but no one would have recognized the modest little rusks in their Easter garb. Another egg, a half cup or more of currants, a few shreds of citron, and a mere suspicion of lemon essence were added, but the process was the same, except that the buns were slightly larger. When they were light enough for baking, Mother would dip a large pair of scissors in flour and cut a deep cross on the top of each. Then when they were quite finished, the glazed surface dry and shining, she would fill the crosses with white icing and perhaps sprinkle a few shreds of citron over the buns. So embellished, they were Hot Cross Buns to be proud of!

Sugar Buns were another form the rusk dough sometimes took. They were made very small, and when light for the oven, a small lump of sugar and a bit of butter were pressed into the center of each. Sugar buns were seldom glazed. They were brushed with butter when the baking was finished and they made delicious tidbits with the afternoon cup of tea.

I think Mother could have made Feather Cake with her eyes closed, for it was in great demand in our large family. It was easily and quickly put together, it could be varied in an infinite number of ways, and, last but by no means least, it was as inexpensive a cake as one could find. Here is her receipt for it:

⌒ FEATHER CAKE ⌒

¼ cup butter	1 cup of milk
2 cups of sugar	1 teaspoon of cream of
3 eggs	tartar
3 cups of flour	Flavoring as preferred
½ teaspoon of soda	

It was that last item, "Flavoring as preferred," that made Feather Cake such a delightful mystery, for Mother liked to surprise us, so we never knew until we had taken our first bite what manner of cake she had made. The batter was mixed in the usual manner—butter softened in a warmed bowl, then creamed quickly and not too fussily with the sugar, eggs slightly beaten, dry ingredients sifted together and whipped into the butter mixture alternately with the milk. Mother could assemble this cake and get it into the oven in ten minutes. Flavoring, as I said, was a matter of choice, sometimes of two choices, for the batter would be divided into two parts, each delicately permeated with its own especial extract or spice to give it distinction. Sometimes it would be vanilla-flavored; again lemon and vanilla were used, both very sparingly; or lemon might be combined with a grating or two of nutmeg; or Mother would stir a little fresh orange or lemon peel into her velvety batter at the last moment to give it a certain zest we all loved.

If a spice cake were in order, a dash each of cinnamon and nutmeg was sifted with the flour, and perhaps a cup of chopped and seeded raisins might go into it also. Father approved of spice cakes, especially if they contained raisins.

We didn't go in very strongly for layer cakes, as I remember, but occasionally Feather Cake would be baked in three shallow pans and put together with thick spreadings of currant or gooseberry jelly, and while still warm, the top layer would be strewn with powdered sugar. Eaten fresh, that simple cake was food for the very gods themselves.

On rare occasions Father and Mother, elegantly attired, went to parties, or to the opera, or to make formal evening calls. Preparations for these social events began early in the day, and were heralded to us children coming home for our midday meal by the sight of Father's best broadcloth hanging on the clothesline in the back yard. Later, when my duties for the day were finished, I would steal up to their room to feast my eyes on my parents' finery, all laid out neatly and painstakingly on the enormous walnut bed with the bunch of walnut grapes ornamenting the headboard.

There was one of Mother's two best grosgrain silk dresses, black or royal purple, according to the tempo of the evening's affair. Both dresses were in the height of style. The purple had an overskirt trimmed heavily with fringe in the same color; the black, a wide ruching of white lace about the high neck and extending all the way down the front of the basque. There were her black kid buttoned shoes and her white silk stockings—the only silk hose she ever owned; her Paisley shawl, with its white center and gay border; her bonnet adorned with an Alsatian bow of straw lace, for which my father had long ago paid twenty-five dollars a yard; and her gloves of purple or white kid to harmonize with her dress, reaching just to the wrist and fastened there with a great pearl clasp. As a last touch there was her embroidered and lace-edged handkerchief, and her gold watch on a long, thin chain. All my mother's cherished finery would be set forth, and on her bureau was the leather box containing her makeup, a piece of white flannel, a cake of lump magnesia and a small bottle of Jockey Club or New Mown Hay perfume to give her an air of genteel refinement.

Father's broadcloth suit, now brushed and freshened; his silk hat, smoothed with a bit of old velvet; his best shirt, hand-sewn by Aunt Sophie, and his tie and kid gloves—all these, in readiness for the evenings festivity, would be carefully arranged on his side of the great bed.

How I would gloat over this array of elegance! No one, I was sure, would ever look more aristocratic, more stylish, than my two parents, when they were ready to mingle with society.

Their home-coming was eagerly anticipated for Mother seldom returned to her family without some souvenir of the occasion—perhaps merely the opera program, over which, the next day, we would pore for hours; perhaps a new crochet or embroidery stitch, for ladies in the eighties took their work with them when they went calling after supper. Occasionally Mother would unfold her delicate hanky and disclose a few bits of cake or sugared almonds or gumdrops, saved from her share of the party refreshments. She never forgot her children, if she could bring them nothing but a cube of loaf sugar all round.

It was at an evening party Mother learned to make a cake then just coming into fashion. Applesauce Cake, although it is still popular, was a mid-Victorian invention, and was fast becoming the rage in the circle in which my parents moved. They ate it at Mrs. Cameron's, liked it and naturally Mother must have the receipt. Immediately it was given a place near the top in our list of specially good cakes.

Mother made it with hot applesauce and often served it fresh from the oven as dessert. Hard sauce made it even better, we discovered, than when it was eaten as a cake, but it was very tasty no matter how or when it was eaten. This is the way it was made:

APPLESAUCE CAKE

1 cup hot applesauce
1 cup brown sugar
¾ teaspoon each soda and
  baking powder
2 cups flour
1 cup seeded and chopped
  raisins
½ cup butter
½ teaspoon each cinnamon
  and nutmeg
¼ teaspoon cloves
1 tablespoon grated lemon
  rind

It was easily made. The flour, spices, soda, and baking powder were sifted together, the lemon rind added to the hot applesauce, the butter and sugar creamed together. Then all the ingredients were combined, and the cake was baked in a square loaf pan in a moderate oven. The baking required from forty-five to sixty minutes. Mother always tested the cake with her clean broom straw when it had been in the oven about three quarters of an hour, to avoid overbaking it. When just exactly right it was a moist tender, luscious sort of cake, though it contained no eggs, which after all was in its favor. If she ever iced it, Mother used brown sugar, which gave a delicious caramel flavor to the whole cake.

Applesauce Cake was entirely too delightful a discovery to keep for her own family, so Mother sent the receipt for it to Aunt Phoebe, who lived in a tiny Canadian town on Lake Erie. Aunt Phoebe was Mother's sister-in-law and a notable cook herself, but Mother was positive she could not have heard of this brand-new cake. What was her astonishment and chagrin, then, to receive from Aunt Phoebe an improvement on Applesauce Cake, which, her letter said, was not at all new to her as she had been making it for at least a year. However, Mother was too good a sport not to give the new cake a trial, and though we hated to admit it, Aunt Phoebe's Honey Applesauce Cake became a close rival of Mrs. Cameron's, and we could never quite decide which one we liked best, though the idea of using honey for sweetening, and adding nuts, did intrigue us tremendously. Here is Aunt Phoebe's receipt:

⌖ HONEY APPLESAUCE CAKE ⌖

⅓ cup butter or lard
¾ cup strained honey
1 cup applesauce (we used it hot)
1 to 1½ cups flour
1 cup chopped and seeded raisins
½ cup chopped nut meats
1 teaspoon soda
1 tablespoon hot water
¼ teaspoon each cloves, ginger, cinnamon, and mace

The shortening was creamed with the honey, and the warm applesauce added. The flour and spices were sifted together and sprinkled over the chopped raisins and nut meats, then all the ingredients were mixed, and the soda, dissolved in the hot water, whipped in at the very last. The cake was baked in a loaf pan for about one hour, and for a finish it was sprinkled with granulated sugar and left in the oven to take on a beautiful glaze.

Somewhere from our English forebears came this receipt for the simple but very tasty little Cornish cakes that my parents, with good friends, enjoyed with their tea on Sunday afternoon. I learned to make them very early in my culinary career and would watch my father with thrilling pride as he made away with far more than his share.

Cornish Cakes

1 tablespoon butter	1 beaten egg
½ cup sugar	1 cup cleaned currants
1 cup sweet milk	2½ cups flour
Pinch of cinnamon	1 teaspoon baking powder

The baking powder was Mother's inspiration. It seemed the original receipt called for no leavening, but in her opinion the cakes were improved by its use. All the ingredients were mixed to a soft dough, kneaded for a few seconds very lightly, then rolled out about one-fourth inch thick and cut in diamonds brushed with beaten egg yolk mixed with a little milk, sprinkled sparingly with sugar and baked in a hot oven. It was fun to make them, and even more fun to split and butter them, hot from the oven, arrange them on a napkin-covered plate and carry them to the parlor or veranda while Anna brought the hot tea. No matter how many times I made them Father always professed to be amazed at my clever performance.

I never knew the history of our delicious Lemon Mace Cake, nor indeed, if it had one, but I remember how delicately scented it was and how pretty it looked, faintly gold, with a thin white icing, when my mother arranged it in our old silver cake basket, which it was my task to keep shining and bright. The cake was simple and easily made.

61

VICTORIAN CAKES

It called for:

୨ LEMON MACE CAKE ୧

½ cup butter
⅔ cup sugar
¼ teaspoon mace
¼ cup lemon juice

2 eggs
1½ teaspoons baking
    powder
2½ cups flour

In making this cake, flour, baking powder, and mace were sifted together. Butter and sugar were creamed, the beaten egg yolks and the lemon juice added. The ingredients were then combined, the egg whites stiffly beaten, and the cake baked in small muffin tins or in a shallow pan and topped with a thin lemon-flavored icing.

Uncle George and Aunt Sophie adored Seed Cake. It was a great favorite of Father's too, and of the English friends who came often to our home, but I don't believe we children ever asked for a second piece. However, it is so closely connected in my memory with the old cake basket and those Sunday afternoon gatherings my parents loved, that I cannot omit it. And really it is a very nice cake. Mother made it from this receipt, combining materials in the usual manner and baking it in a moderate oven. It was never iced, merely strewn with fine sugar.

୨ SEED CAKE ୧

¼ cup butter
2 cups sugar
4 eggs
1 cup milk

3 cups flour
2 teaspoons caraway seeds
2 teaspoons baking powder
¼ cup finely shaved citron

Doughnuts, lightsome, nutty, twisted, or in rings, were one of our dessert delights, and Mother made them to perfection. I remember how spicily good the whole place did smell as we youngsters bounded noisily in from school on crisp winter days, and how ravishingly good the freshly made cakes looked, piled high in the sturdy old brown crock, and how even better they tasted, still warm and sugary, to two healthy, hungry girls.

My share—I always begged for the puffy little "fried holes," as we called them—was invariably carried to the attic, where, if the milk room was crowded, the winter's supply of apples was stored. There, with *English Orphans* or *Lady Audley's Secret*, neither considered quite the reading for a young girl, I would munch and nibble, first a bite of Russet or Northern Spy, then a sugar-dredged "hole," reading as long as my eyes could see, whereupon I would make my way, appetite unabated, to the bountiful supper table. And later, when my lessons had been learned, I would manage to eat still another doughnut or two with my before-going-to-bed mug of milk. And did I have nightmares? Never! Life was too interesting, too filled with pleasant things to do or to eat. Tomorrow I might go skating on Ten Mile Ditch, the capacious pockets in my coat filled with doughnuts. No place for nightmares in such a busy life as mine!

Mother's doughnut receipt came from New England via an aunt who had lived there at some time in her eventful life. It went like this:

⌒ DOUGHNUTS ⌒

1 tablespoon butter	½ teaspoon salt
1 cup sugar	3 cups of flour
1 egg	3 teaspoons baking powder
1 teaspoon cinnamon	Milk to make a soft dough
½ teaspoon lemon extract	

The method of putting these ingredients together was not unusual. There was but one trick to the whole process, and that was to keep the dough as soft as possible, in order that the cakes might be feathery and delicate. Mother used to make up her dough, roll it out on the floured breadboard, and cut every one, before she fried even a single "hole." In this way the cakes had an opportunity to rise just a little before the hot fat began its action on them. It eliminated, too, the usual trotting back and forth from cutting board to doughnut kettle, and the danger of scorching a few of the precious cakes.

It was good fun to watch the frying process when Mother made doughnuts. Our kettle was a family heirloom; it was wide and shallow and set quite flat. Anna half filled it with lard when the doughnut making began, and set it on the hottest part of the stove, so that it was quite ready for Mother's frying when the cakes were all cut, some of them in rings with the traditional hole in the center, others in diamond shapes, still others like small gridirons with crinkly edges made by a jigging iron. We each had our favorites, mine the puffy balls, the crisp fried "holes." Kitty preferred those with the crinkly edges.

Sometimes, when the days were very cold and stormy, Mother would permit us to carry our lunch to school, though always with some misgivings and protests, for she preferred to have her flock about her, to see that we ate properly of the good, warm dinner she and Anna always had in readiness for us at noon.

But we children felt quite differently about the matter, and would have thoroughly enjoyed sitting about the old school stove with the other youngsters every day of the year, unpacking our hard-boiled eggs, and half-frozen sandwiches and setting our bottle of milk to thaw—perhaps even trading doughnuts for cookies or gingerbread for mince pie, just as they did, and afterwards, perhaps, playing some wild game up and down the aisles. But Mother had her own ideas about such matters, and therefore, unless it was snowing and blowing what Anna called a regular blizzard, we always started homeward at the stroke of noon, Mother or Anna meeting us half way.

On those days, however, when the kitchen clock foretold very rough weather, Father was on our side, and we trudged to school, buoyantly lugging Aunt Sophie's brown-covered basket between us. Usually on these occasions Millie Andress hailed us, carrying her tin pail and we made our way through the storm together. Now and then the sidewalks would be so hidden by the snowdrifts that we walked the fence rails to keep from being lost, and sometimes one of us would lose her footing and fall so deeply into a snowbank that it was a hard matter to pull her out, but it was all in the nature of adventure and we welcomed and loved it.

Our lunch basket was the envy of the other children, for Mother and Anna seemed to have the idea that the lunch they prepared for us would be the last meal we would ever eat, and accordingly it must be the best. Such piles of sandwiches and turnovers! Such handsome hard-boiled eggs!—for Anna took out the yolks, mashed them with melted butter and cream, seasoned them nicely, and put them back with some sort of a twist on top that made them shine among all the other boiled eggs around the stove.

But it was Mother's Drop Cakes, I believe, that used to make the deepest and certainly the most lasting impression. She made them quickly, often while we were dressing and getting ourselves into the multitudinous wrappings considered necessary for our journey. We wore Father's woolen socks over our shoes; high buckled overshoes lined with red flannel over the socks; and cardigan jackets, which I think Emil must have donated, under our heavy winter coats, with old plaid shawls over the coats. Hoods which Anna crocheted for us, we always wore in cold weather; but on these bitter days we had heavy scarfs over the hoods and wrapped round our throats. Mittens—as many as we could get on—and then, as a last touch,

Emily would often tie thick veils over our faces, but these we removed as soon as we were out of sight of the house. Bad enough to have to wear Father's socks, but veils——! How we should have been ridiculed at school!

But to return to the Drop Cakes, which Mother made so frequently and so well and so varied. Her receipt as I have interpreted it was:

DROP CAKES

1 cup shortening	1 cup hot water
1 cup brown sugar	1 teaspoon soda
1 egg slightly beaten	Spices or flavoring to taste
1 cup molasses	Flour for a stiff batter

The soda was dissolved in the hot water, the shortening creamed with the sugar, then all the other ingredients were turned in, the flour gradually, to avoid getting the dough too stiff. For flavoring Mother used cinnamon and nutmeg, or extract of vanilla or lemon. Sometimes she added a few raisins or currants or chopped nut meats, or perhaps a few spoonfuls of jam or marmalade. They were always different and always good. She dropped the cakes from the end of a spoon on greased tins and baked them in a moderate oven. For very special treats she would scatter coconut or nut meats over the cakes just before putting them in the oven.

If Emily happened to be in the kitchen, our cakes were frequently iced. Then we could have traded them for anything we wanted, from any lunch basket or pail in the school, for they were certainly at a premium.

Poetry and Gingerbread

UNCLE GEORGE was not only a poet, he was quite famous on another count as well. A great artist once painted his picture and we had all gone to see it at the Exposition. There it hung in its handsome gilt frame, along with the mayor and other notables, and it was really Uncle George, though in the catalogue, printed very clearly, was the title the artist had given it: "Life's Autumn." But no one could have mistaken the portrait. It was Uncle George to the life, aristocratic features, the nose slightly red; white tufts of hair like wings over the neat ears; mild, somewhat watery, but very blue eyes under bushy white brows; close-cut, snow-white mustache veiling but not concealing a mouth that some of the relatives considered selfish, but which Uncle George and Aunt Sophie thought beautifully shaped.

Uncle George's favorite diversion for several months thereafter was nonchalantly to station himself near the picture, where the comments of the visitors to the gallery would be quite audible. It was startling how greatly the picture resembled him. Many persons, mostly ladies, remarked it, he used to tell us at supper.

In Father's judgment the portrait episode ruined whatever of usefulness Uncle George might theretofore have possessed. To be sure, he wrote a poem every day of his life. That, to my hard-working, practical parent, was bad enough, but now he had been painted and exhibited— well, he was finished, and that was that.

Uncle George, however, took his poetry very seriously. True, the world had never heard of him, at least not directly, but could anyone who had ever read an advertisement for the "Empire Parlor Bedstead," the ancestor of all folding beds, have missed his daily poem extolling that useful article? His poem, written with such fervor, such pathos, such—well, everything that a poet could give— could anyone at all, whether in need of a bedstead or not, have overlooked it? Decidedly not, thought Uncle George.

The payment for all this fire and effort was small indeed, far too small to afford Uncle George and Aunt Sophie a living consistent with their birth, upbringing, and Uncle George's genius. So to the home of their favorite niece they came, quite naturally, and there made themselves thoroughly comfortable and at ease.

That is, Aunt Sophie, gentle, blundering, fat, deaf Aunt Sophie, was comfortable and happy as the day was long, helping Mother with her endless housekeeping tasks, sewing fine seams, puttering about in the kitchen and eating three generous meals a day—meals that included all the good things she loved, the best cuts of the roast, the most delectable portion of the dessert, the first glass of port. Yes, Aunt Sophie, bless her kind old heart, after a precarious existence of many years with her poet-husband, was at peace with the world at last.

Uncle George was not always as patient as he might have been. He railed at fate for making him second or third or fourth in a family not quite rich enough to establish even the eldest son as eldest sons in the Hargreave clan had every right to be established. He railed at the newspapers and wrote impatient letters to the editors on the quality of verse they presented to a long-suffering public; he railed, mildly, of course, at his adoring old wife for her failure to bring him at least a modest dowry; but most of all, he railed at Father's selection of his clothing, which, sturdy, durable, and comfortable as it might be, was "not the type a gentleman, especially a Hargreave, should be seen wearing."

But on the whole, both Uncle George and Aunt Sophie fitted into our household very well. To be sure, there were occasional clashes. Uncle George objected wrathfully to our games of hide and seek in the hayloft, where he, snugly stowed away in a corner, far from the world which he complained was always too much with him was striving to compose his poem.

Aunt Sophie, in her good-natured way, was forever letting the cat out of the bag when one or the other of us had some secret project on foot; and that was very irritating, we thought, and we often said so, too, sometimes very saucily.

These flurries were soon over, however, and everything quickly restored to its usual tranquillity. We children really loved the old couple, especially Aunt Sophie, who was always ready to sew a button on one's shoe, mend a torn dress, or make some of her own especial cookies for us. She was rather a lavish cook, this Aunt Sophie, and everything she made tasted specially good because of the extra little dabs of butter or sugar or cream she invariably introduced into her receipts. Her Shrewsbury Cakes were marvels of richness, as the amount of butter to be used was left to the judgment of the cook, and Aunt Sophie was a generous judge. Here is the old receipt from her treasured collection:

69

VICTORIAN CAKES

SHREWSBURY CAKES

2 cups sugar	Cinnamon and nutmeg as
3 eggs	you like
12 cups flour	Butter to make a proper
A little rose water	paste

Not all the flour was used in mixing the cooky dough. Aunt Sophie usually put one cup aside for her pastry board and rolling pin; the rest, sifted with the spices, she mixed with the sugar and the well-beaten eggs and stirred the mixture well; then added the butter, which had been slowly melting to a liquid state on the back of the stove. Pouring the butter very gradually and stirring the paste constantly with a wooden paddle, she soon reduced it to a workable consistency. Next the rose water was added, also very deliberately and with much tasting. Aunt Sophie loved to taste as much as did her small nieces, so we were thoroughly in accord. When in our opinion, the dough was flavored exactly as it should be, it was turned out on the floured pastry board, kneaded for a few moments, rolled thin as paper, and cut in large scalloped cakes.

Aunt Sophie often allowed me to put the cakes in the greased pans, which I did very importantly. When baked to a lovely golden brown, some of them we would ornament with hickory-nut meats, others might be sprinkled lightly with granulated sugar, and a few Aunt Sophie would bake specially for Uncle George, strewing the dough for them thickly with the caraway seeds he adored.

No one in the house could make a gingerbread that came anywhere near Aunt Sophie's. It was so tender, so mellow, and so spicy that we never tired of it, but I think the story that went with it intrigued us all as much as the substantial and satisfying cake itself. We were always a great family for stories, and if by any chance they related to one of our favorite cakes, they pleased us so much the more.

Aunt Sophie called this cake "Dream Gingerbread," because, so she declared quite positively, her mother, who was my mother's grandmother, had made the cake in a beautiful dream one night, and waking, was so impressed by the quality of her dream cake that then and there she flew to her kitchen in her nightcap and gown and made a cake exactly like the one in her dream. And so delighted were she and her family with the result that Dream Gingerbread immediately became the standard for all gingerbreads, among the entire kith and kin and the fame of it spread even into neighboring counties and cities.

I like that story today quite as well as I did when Aunt Sophie told it to me, and whether it was authentic or not, Aunt Sophie's Dream Gingerbread was second to none. Here is the receipt:

⟨⟩ DREAM GINGERBREAD ⟨⟩

1 cup shortening, butter and lard mixed is best	1 tablespoon ginger
	½ teaspoon each cinnamon and mace
1 cup brown sugar	
1 cup molasses	1 teaspoon soda
1 cup sour or buttermilk	3½ to 4 cups flour
2 eggs	

Aunt Sophie put shortening, sugar, and molasses in a bowl, which she set over the simmering tea-kettle; when quite warm, she beat the ingredients to a cream with her wooden paddle. Following this she broke the eggs in one at a time with more beating. The flour, measured usually by one of her eager helpers, was mixed with the spices and soda before being sifted; then about three cups of it were added to the butter and molasses mixture, alternately with the milk, and the batter examined critically. Sometimes a "try cake" was made to ascertain whether it was stiff enough; if not, more of the flour was added very cautiously, for the tenderness of the cake depended on having the batter exactly right, neither too thin nor too thick.

Dream Gingerbread might be baked in a round or square loaf-cake pan, in a sheet, or in muffin tins, as the occasion seemed to demand, and Aunt Sophie had innumerable ways of varying it and dressing it up, so that we never tired of it. Sometimes she iced it with a simple paste of brown sugar and sour cream, or she strewed it with powdered sugar as she took it from the oven, or added bits of preserved ginger from Uncle George's private jar imported from China, or raisins might take the place of the ginger, or chopped nuts enrich it. Aunt Sophie's Dream Gingerbread was always a treat, plain or embellished, hot or cold. We often ate it for dessert, oven-fresh, with cottage cheese, or topped with a generous tablespoonful of Mother's Devonshire Clotted Cream. Father relished it with a dish of fresh sugared currants from his own garden, or if it were winter, with currants from the same source made into jam.

Tipsy Parson, a very old dish which Mother remembered from her own childhood, was one of Aunt Sophie's most famous specialties, an ethereal dessert, built on a sponge-cake foundation, which, when it was finished, looked more like an air castle than any sort of a parson, tipsy or otherwise. It was a royal dessert, reserved for extra special company, men of affairs from Montreal or Toronto who came now and then to discuss business with Father, or for Professor Nightingale of our high school, or for someone of equal greatness.

Aunt Sophie always seemed to feel a sense of importance when she made Tipsy Parson. No standing around begging for tastes was tolerated, although, after all, the dessert was a simple one. First she would make the sponge-cake by this formula:

∽ SPONGECAKE ∽

3 eggs	¼ teaspoon salt
1 cup sugar	Flavoring, usually vanilla
¼ cup water	1 teaspoon baking powder
1 cup sifted flour	

The eggs were beaten to a fluffy foam, the sugar then added and both beaten vigorously until like a batter. The flour was twice sifted with the baking powder and salt; and the water was added to the egg and sugar; then the flour, baking powder, and salt combination folded in, and the batter turned into a round tube pan about eight inches in diameter. Aunt Sophie preferred a moderate oven for this spongecake, for she never liked it to become too brown.

Next the cake, slightly warm, was placed in our best glass dish, where Madeira wine was drizzled generously all over it. It was then set away in a cold place while Aunt Sophie made a rich boiled custard flavored delicately with vanilla. About half an hour before dinner she would bring out the spongecake, drizzle a little more Madeira over it, and stick it quite full of blanched almonds. Then she would smother it in the delicious chilled custard and fill the center with apple or currant or raspberry jelly, cut in cubes. Whipped cream, slightly sweetened and flavored with Madeira, was piled in peaks over the whole dish, and bits of the red jelly set here and there over the cream, like jewels. It was a sumptuous dish!

My impression is that Tipsy Parson was an English dessert, for Aunt Sophie had a great store of receipts and other cookery lore from the Homeland, conveyed to Canada by visiting friends and, after the roving manner of all good receipts, finally reaching the little town on Lake Erie where she had spent her youth, and where Mother was born. Mother's receipts were also typical of England, but Aunt Sophie's were older and, in a manner, more interesting, for nearly all of them had fascinating stories connected with their origins; and Aunt Sophie loved to tell these tales as she padded about the kitchen assembling her materials, sifting flour, beating eggs, and grinding spices. Her deafness was never a handicap when she chose to tell a story, but what embarrassing moments she often caused the grown folks, especially Uncle George, by her interpretation of some of theirs! She was a merry old lady, too, and could laugh as heartily at her blunders as anyone else. We children loved her anecdotes, and it made no difference to us if she repeated them a thousand times.

One of Aunt Sophie's most delectable cakes was Sally Lunn, real old fashioned Sally Lunn, made, she claimed, by the receipt invented by Sally herself. Sally, so went Aunt Sophie's legend, used to peddle her cakes, neatly covered in a wicker basket, through the streets and highways of Bath, a hundred years or more before; and she had such a pretty way of calling her wares that a baker-musician, hearing her, was so greatly attracted and impressed that he bought her receipt and went into the business of making the tempting cakes himself. He did even more, for he set Sally's little ditty to music, and made up a song about her and her wares which became so popular that soon everybody was singing it. In no time at all the cakes became so famous that the baker-musician had to trundle them about in wheelbarrows, and he eventually made a great fortune just from his Sally Lunns. To make the story complete and give it a happy ending, Aunt Sophie, who was a romantic old soul was of the opinion that the baker-musician should have married Sally Lunn and lived happily with her ever afterward.

Whether he did or not, Sally's receipt lives, in Great Aunt Sophie's slanting writing, in a discolored old copybook which is one of my greatest treasures. In the old receipt all the ingredients are measured by tumbler or half tumblerful, except salt and soda, which go by pinches and double pinches. New milk, fresh from the cow, and home-made yeast are demanded. All very interesting, naturally, but a cake made by my translated receipt is very, very good, and far easier to make, so here is the modern version of Great Aunt Sophie's historic Sally Lunn:

⟨⟩ SALLY LUNN ⟨⟩

4 eggs	¾ cup warm water
½ cup melted butter	½ cake yeast
4 tablespoons sugar	4 cups flour (approximate)
1 teaspoon salt	⅛ teaspoon soda
1 cup warm milk	

Dissolve the yeast in the warm water, heat the milk lukewarm, sift the flour, and melt the butter. Then proceed as Aunt Sophie did, in that old kitchen of ours so long ago. Beat the eggs and add the melted butter, sugar, salt and warm milk; sift the soda with the flour and combine with the other mixture, whipping in the dissolved yeast. Gradually add the flour; it may not be necessary to use it all, for the batter should be as soft as possible. Beat thoroughly, then cover the bowl with a clean towel and set away for an hour or two to become light. When it is bubbly and full of little holes, stir the batter down and turn it into a well-buttered tube pan and leave to rise once more, then bake a full hour in a moderately hot oven.

Aunt Sophie started her Sally Lunns in the middle of the morning if they were to be served warm for tea, and she always took very good care that the slices were generously spread with good fresh butter. If by chance the cake was not all eaten at its first serving, she would toast it for the next afternoon's tea table. It went superbly with Mother's ginger pears or peach butter.

Chelsea Buns were likewise specialties of Aunt Sophie's which had an interesting history attached to them. They were older than Sally Lunns, and quite as romantic, in our youthful opinions. A Mrs. Hand in Chelsea made excellent buns, so excellent that royalty, in the persons of George II and Queen Caroline, often paid visits to her shop to eat the fresh buns. George III, when he came to the throne, followed the custom of his ancestor, and Queen Charlotte even carried things so far as to present a silver mug to Mrs. Hand. This news of course was spread abroad, and the buns immediately became so tremendously popular that Mrs. Hand had to issue a proclamation that hereafter the strain on her nerves being entirely too great, she would make the buns but one day in the week. We thought that a lovely story, and we thought Mrs. Hand's Chelsea Buns quite as good as Sally Lunns. Here is Aunt Sophie's reconstructed receipt for these dainties:

CHELSEA BUNS

1 cup milk	½ teaspoon cinnamon
½ cup butter	3 egg yolks
½ cup sugar	Flour as necessary—about
¼ cup currants	three cups
¼ yeast cake	¼ cup shredded citron

The milk was scalded, butter added, then cooled to lukewarm, when the yeast, crumbled in small pieces, was added, with a portion of the flour. This was well beaten and set in a sheltered place to become very light. The egg yolks were then beaten with the sugar to a light, fluffy foam and added to the batter with the well-washed and dried currants, the cinnamon and citron, and more flour, as required to make a dough stiff enough for kneading. After this had been thoroughly done, the dough was set away to rise a second time. Then it was rolled out in a sheet about one-half inch thick, cut in rounds with a large biscuit cutter, placed on buttered baking tins about two inches apart, set in a warm place until very light, and then baked about thirty-five minutes in a moderately hot oven.

When Aunt Sophie took her Chelsea Buns from the oven she rubbed them all over with butter, and they looked and smelled heavenly. I could quite understand why the two King Georges had so loved to visit Mrs. Hand's shop, and always, when I ate my own fresh, spicy bun, I pictured kings and queens, gold crowns on their heads, stepping out from Mrs. Hand's bun shop munching their Chelsea Buns.

But Aunt Sophie's quaint stories of Sally Lunn and her cakes, and Mrs. Hand with her silver mug, paled before that of Simon and Nelly and their strange hodge-podge of a cake which Mother's down-at-the-heels old cookbook called Simnel Cake, and of which it said, "These cakes are of great antiquity; they are quite indigestible."

Uncle George was the discoverer and exponent of the anecdote, just as Aunt Sophie was the interpreter and executor of the receipt, and their discussions and disputes about the cake, its history, and to whom should go the glory of its renaissance, were so appropriate to the occasion and so amusing I have never forgotten them; nor how red their poor old faces would grow as they argued, Uncle George in carefully chosen words, Aunt Sophie waving the wooden paddle and not hearing a word he uttered. But here is the legend, invented so far back in England's history that no one knows, or perhaps cares, just when or where it originated.

Simnel Cakes were a Mothers' Day offering, for England had a Mothers' Day of her own long before America was discovered. Mothering Sunday they called it, far back in the dim ages, and it was the custom for all good girls and worthy young men to present their mothers, not with a carnation, but with a cake, on that Sunday. The tale Uncle George unearthed of the origin of the cake is perhaps even older than the cakes themselves. In fact, it very probably goes back to the first Mothers' Day of all. Simon and Nelly, so it goes, decided to make a very fine cake, putting into it all the rich things they could gather together, and while in the process of making it, a discussion arose between them as to how it should be cooked. Simon was all for boiling it, but Nelly, equally positive, declared that for such a wonderful cake as theirs, only baking was to be considered.

The argument raged furiously, until, as neither would give in an iota and the cake seemed destined never to be cooked at all, they decided both to boil and to bake it. Furthermore, as it would prove such a novelty, they would give it both their names as well. So "Simnel" it has been ever since, and boiled and baked it has also been ever since. Made after the original receipt, Simnel cakes must have been very strange concoctions. Uncle George solemnly told of a lady from foreign parts who, presented with one of these astonishing cakes on Mothering Sunday, used it for a footstool for many months before she realized what it was.

In Mother's old cookbook the receipt for making Simnel Cake directs that first a yeast-risen dough, colored and flavored well with saffron, be made. This is then to be flattened well and filled with a rich plum-cake mixture, very stiff and unyielding but overflowing with candied peels, raisins of the sun, spices, and other good things. Then the whole thing is tied up in a cloth, plum-puddingwise, and boiled four hours, after which the cloth is removed, and the mass of dough and fruit is rubbed all over with beaten eggs and baked four more hours. "When finished," so the old receipt ends, "the crust should be as hard as though made of wood."

Aunt Sophie's Simnel was quite different. True, she

followed tradition as far as her reasoning would permit, but she first steamed the cake in place of the prescribed boiling, and then baked it in a slow oven. The following receipt is hers, slightly Americanized as to measurements by myself, but still Aunt Sophie's Simnel:

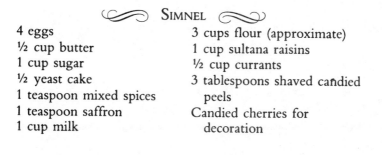

SIMNEL

4 eggs	3 cups flour (approximate)
½ cup butter	1 cup sultana raisins
1 cup sugar	½ cup currants
½ yeast cake	3 tablespoons shaved candied
1 teaspoon mixed spices	peels
1 teaspoon saffron	Candied cherries for
1 cup milk	decoration

The milk is scalded with the saffron, then cooled to lukewarm and strained. The yeast is crumbled into it, butter and sugar creamed together and added with a portion of the flour sifted with the spices. Eggs are beaten in one at a time; then more flour, with the fruit, is whipped in. The mixture should be quite stiff but in no wise a dough. When it was well mixed Aunt Sophie turned it into a liberally buttered mold and put it in a warm place. When it had risen to double its bulk, she covered it closely, steamed it for one and a half hours, and baked it in a slow oven for another hour. When cool, it was iced with a thin paste made of very fine sugar, cream, and a few drops of lemon or vanilla extract, and decorated with the candied cherries, and perhaps a few shreds of green citron.

Aunt Sophie always made several of these handsome and very delicious cakes to send to friends at Easter. Uncle George, in his best bib and tucker, would deliver them, and probably took as much credit for the gift as he dared. Mother heard that he never lost an opportunity of telling

the classic story of the cake and repeating the old rhyme—
Herrick's, I believe:

> I'le to thee a Simnell bring,
>
> 'Gainst thou go'st a *mothering,*
>
> So that, when she blesseth thee,
>
> Half that blessing thou'lt give me.

Trust Uncle George to know his poetry!

Father's Lady Friends

Like All Irishmen, Father had a way with him. Moreover, he was handsome, as good looks were in the eighties; hazel eyes, face smooth except for the Dundrearies that were carefully brushed and combed every morning; mouth large, but well shaped; hair wearing a bit on the temples, perhaps, but still thick and virile and of a deep chestnut brown; tall of stature and stately of bearing—altogether a fine figure of a man, with a mind worthy his comely appearance.

Demanding he was, but kind and indulgent to a degree. But let no one impose on his good nature, that he would not suffer. He was the "boss," as Emily constantly reminded us, and what the boss said was law and gospel. Only Emily ever defied him, but she was his favorite and pal. Emily understood his jokes, which were frequently too obscure for the rest of us; she supported and abetted him in all his undertakings, ministered to him when sick headaches laid him low, shielded him from annoyances, cooked his favorite dishes for him; and on those summer evenings when it was his fancy to ride through Lincoln Park and along Lake Shore Drive with all his daughters, it was always Emily's horse which cantered beside his own. The rest of us meekly followed, guiding our mounts as best we might with our sister waving encouragement to us as we all swept along in our flowing habits (mine, I remember, trimmed ornately with little brass buttons like gold dollars), Father looking proudly ahead, his Dundrearies floating in the breeze. It was not surprising that a man of Father's presence held great attraction for the ladies. Every unattached female who came into our home, and many, I fear, who were already safely married, had her flirtatious eye on him. Visitors, pensioners, clients, all fell before Father's Irish charm; but he, to do him justice, was to all appearances quite unconscious of his conquests, while Mother was merely amused, and we children thought it uproariously funny that Uncle George should tease an old man like our father about his lady friends.

After all, we would have missed them sadly, those admirers of his, had they taken themselves out of our lives, for strangely enough nearly every one of them was either a warm friend of my mother's or a useful personage in our household, whose coming we all welcomed heartily and whose going we mourned. Their contributions to our good times were highly appreciated. They brought us gossip of the world beyond our door with which they were familiar.

There was Mrs. Alcott, who came for several weeks each spring and fall to help clothe us for the coming season. Her advent was heralded by bustling preparations. Mother made all-day trips to Field and Leiter's dry-goods store to lay in a supply of materials for our garments——plaids, alpacas, cashmeres, lawns, book muslins, dimities, and ginghams; and pattern books, piles of pattern books, which were studied diligently by the whole female portion of the family; fresh supplies of sewing cotton, silk, hooks and eyes, pins and needles, tape, and what not, she laid in, too, for the campaign. The sewing room would be swept and garnished, and old sheets fastened over the carpet. Emil sharpened and oiled the scissors and shears, and Father helped the good work along by putting the Florence sewing machine in tiptop trim. Mrs. Alcott always preferred to be on hand during this operation, in order she said, to direct it, but Aunt Sophie declared she made eyes at Father as he shortened straps, adjusted the tension, tuck marker, and ruffler, all the time casting merry, bantering remarks her way.

Mrs. Alcott, throughout all the years that I remember her, described herself as "fair, fat, and forty." Her hair, a sort of faded auburn, was frizzed on hot slate pencils every afternoon before Father's return from his office. She had gentle blue eyes and a very high color, and wore clothes and shoes so tight that she was in a constant state of having "a rush of blood to the head." But once Father was safely on his way to town in the morning, she loosened her stays, donned a wrapper and an old pair of Mother's slippers, and got to the business of the day in no time at all, chattering of new styles in overskirts, whether puffing or pleating was coming in, how Mrs. Cook looked in her blue taffeta from Paris which Mrs. Alcott had been called in "practically to make over," and a hundred other topics, with occasionally a tearful reference to Kitty and Mr. Alcott, her daughter and husband, dead many years before.

At luncheon, always prepared with especial care to include some pet dish of hers, Mrs. Alcott's conversation would turn to cookery, and many a bit of household lore or receipt for a grand new dish would transfer itself from the notebook where addresses, measurements, data about her clients, and receipts were all dashed down in tangled confusion, to Mother's old copybook that was also a clearing house for odds and ends of miscellaneous information.

Always on one of the evenings while Mrs. Alcott was with us, Emil would uncover and polish the carriage, fit fresh candles in the lamps, and Father, Mrs. Alcott, and

Mother, and perhaps one or two of us youngsters, would drive to Rose Hill Cemetery, where Mr. Alcott and Kitty had been resting so many years. On other evenings the Democrat wagon would take as many of us as could pile into it, Mrs. Alcott on the front seat beside Father, through the park or down the Lake Shore Drive. These excursions were always followed by a bite to eat, accompanied by much pleasantry on Father's part and coquettish blushes on Mrs. Alcott's.

All in all it was good fun to have her with us. She petted us as children, advised us as we grew up, and sympathized with us always. She was constantly prophesying that we would all be "heart smashers," an embarrassing statement and a hateful one if made in the presence of Uncle George, for he never forgot it nor did he ever neglect an occasion to remind us of it gleefully. But she was kind and affectionate and one could tell her anything. When I, at sixteen, was secretly in love with a young newspaperman, she was the one person in whom I felt I could confide. I remember she was making me a dress of crushed strawberry silk with panniers at the time, and as she puckered and pinned and measured, she whispered more than once, "We must make this pretty so the *Evening News* will like you in it." And then later, when I married an entirely different man, she made my wedding dress and tactfully forbore even to mention the *Evening News*.

Straight to our kitchen from Mrs. Alcott's old home in New England came the receipt for Marble Cake, and it was tested faithfully and given a place in Mother's collection of cakes suitable for company, and extra nice for family fare. Mrs. Alcott herself made it on several occasions, with Emily as helper and the rest of us, more or less, hanging over the mixing bowls and spoons. Marble Cake was made in two parts, which was novel and interesting. One was light, the other dark, and the batters were arranged in a buttered tube pan by large spoonfuls, light and dark alternating, and the cake was baked in a moderate oven about three quarters of an hour. Mrs. Alcott confessed it was the one and only cake she could make successfully, as dressmaking was her forte; but she was so neat-handed and skillful, and her Marble Cake was so delicious that we decided she was entirely too humble. But here is her receipt:

MARBLE CAKE

Light Part	*Dark Part*
½ cup butter	1 cup brown sugar
1½ cups sugar	¼ cup butter
½ cup milk	½ cup milk
2 cups flour	1½ cups flour
4 egg whites	2 squares cooking chocolate
2 teaspoons baking powder	4 egg yolks
½ teaspoon vanilla	Dash of cinnamon
	¼ teaspoon soda
	1 teaspoon baking powder
	½ teaspoon vanilla

Each part of the cake was mixed separately, flour sifted with the leavening, butter and sugar creamed, and so on. The chocolate was melted in a small saucepan set in a larger one of hot water. When Mrs. Alcott began spooning the batters in the pan, first a spoonful or two of light, then one of dark, it was quite exciting, but it was even more exciting when she took her cake from the oven, fragrant and delicious, and iced it. The operation went something like this: first a thick white coating of frosting was applied evenly all over the top and sides, and the cake was set aside to dry. Then she would drizzle melted chocolate all over it in streaks, in order further to carry out the marble effect. At times, if the white icing had not entirely set, the chocolate would blend into it in a very realistic way, which was greatly admired.

VICTORIAN CAKES

Miss Dexter, Miss Lizzie Dexter, was another flame of my father's whether he was aware of the fact or not. Miss Dexter was an Irish gentlewoman of uncertain age with whom Mother had conceived a great friendship at the time of the great Chicago Fire. Miss Dexter's family, having lived on the West side, had not suffered, but we on the North side had lost everything we possessed, Father and Mother barely escaping with their lives. After it was over, committees were formed to investigate and aid the Fire sufferers, and in this way Miss Dexter met my mother, and their friendship, thus started, continued through the years.

In her early youth Miss Dexter had been a beauty, a fact she could never forget. She still wore the delicate mauves, rosebud pinks, and forget-me-not blues that in her teens and twenties had been pronounced her colors. Her hair, still brown, but showing traces of gray, fell in ringlets over her forehead, and she prided herself on her tiny waist. She was our favorite guest. For all her ladylike ways, she had a hearty laugh, enjoyed a refined joke, and always, when she came to visit, brought us youngsters gifts of chocolate mice with wooly tails. She was fascinating, too, because of the great variety of things she could do. There was nothing in the world, or so it seemed, that had the power to stump Miss Dexter. She painted beautiful plaques with scenes from Melrose Abbey, or pansies with curling stems and tendrils; she made wax flowers and autumn leaves that rebuked nature; she could mend, recondition, make over, or in prove almost anything one could think of, from a piece of fine lace to an old master.

One job of hers I shall never forget. She restored our treasured wax fruit! On the marble center table in our before-the-Fire parlor had stood the *pièce de résistance* of our home, a beautiful faïence basket heaped with an assortment of the most luscious fruit ever seen outside Eden— grapes, purple, red and green; yellow pears; glowing peaches; a halved orange, more than true to life; wine-hued plums; and enormous scarlet strawberries on which perched a large and handsome bee. At the side of the basket reposed a section of watermelon oozing realistic brown seeds, that even to look at fairly ravished one. A large, clear glass shade protected the wax fruit from dust and vandals. As a tiny child I used to spend hours walking round and round that table admiring, longing; and a favorite game with us youngsters had been one of our own invention called "Choose a Fruit."

By tremendous effort Mother had saved the wax fruit and the shade from the fire. I think she buried it along with her Florence sewing machine and the jams and jellies, in a deep pit Anna's father dug for them in our back yard on La Salle Street. Months afterward our treasure was restored to us, but in sorry shape. Mother was almost ashamed to have it seen, until Miss Dexter restored it.

What a piece of work that was! The dining-room table was covered thickly with newspapers; wax molds, powdered colors, and brushes were set forth. Clustered ringlets over her blue eyes, dainty skirts spread decently and alluringly about her, mauve ribbon strings to her sheer apron, Miss Dexter, alluring and coquettish, sat brightly before all this paraphernalia, daintily touching a wax peach, or molding a new rind for the orange, or shyly asking Father's help with a bit of difficult gluing, and blushing frantically if by the remotest chance their fingers touched. We children hung over her by the hour as she worked, for which Father might have thanked us, but I fear Miss Dexter did not.

She would shriek with laughter at his witticisms, flatter him outrageously, ask his advice about her minute investments, and defer to him modestly and humbly. Once at dinner when all the grownups had partaken of Rhine wine with ice and sugar, Father announced that he had selected Miss Dexter for his second wife, which so excited and embarrassed her that she rushed headlong from the table and my mother was obliged to follow and soothe her. After that, I think she always regarded us children with a slight air of proprietorship, which we gratefully accepted.

Miss Dexter's contribution to our store of receipts was rich, for she could make any number of Scotch and Irish dishes and make them well, too. Father particularly enjoyed a sort of stew which she called haricot of mutton; Uncle George constantly asked her for collops, but I think she was most famous in our family for her cakes. One especially we preferred to all others. Its name had a glamorous sound, and the cake was uncommonly good. She called it "The King's Shoe Laces," and she made it this way:

◁∽ THE KING'S SHOE LACES ∽▷

First she separated the yolks and whites of three eggs, and sifted a cup of flour with the "merest smidge" of baking powder, explaining, as she did so, that it was quite out of order and that Ma would never allow her to do it at home, but she thought it an improvement, and besides it was, after all, just the "merest smidge." The egg yolks were beaten stiff and about three fourths of a cup of sugar added; then the beating continued, Miss Baxter's ringlets shaking merrily as the fork dashed the egg yolks and sugar to a fluffy, yellow foam. For flavoring she preferred two tablespoons of orange-flower water with the grated rind of a lemon, but she could manage with a teaspoon of lemon extract plus the lemon peel and enough water to make two tablespoons full. Next the flour was folded in delicately, and finally the whites of the eggs, whipped to snowy peaks, were added. The batter was spread thin in a buttered and floured pan and baked in a moderate oven. When it was still hot the cake was cut in long, narrow strips and dusted with powdered sugar. And how good they were with a glass of cold milk or lemonade, or in winter with hot cocoa, for luncheon!

Real romance entered our lives with the arrival of Miss Henrietta Smythe from the little Canadian village where Father and Mother had met, fallen in love, and married. Miss Smythe, on her way to spend a winter with a nephew in Kansas, decided to break her long journey in Chicago and, as Mother had often pressed her to do, spend a fortnight at our home. It all sounded very casual and quite regular to us, until Uncle George began teasing my parents about her coming. Such mysterious hints, such sly allusions as he interjected into his conversation! We could make nothing of it all and were simply consumed with curiosity, which no one would satisfy. Father and Mother merely laughed, perhaps a trifle self-consciously, and told us to go on with our dinner, or study our lessons, or mind our own affairs—just as though any affair that seemed to involve them was not ours as well!

Finally Emily contrived to coax the secret from Aunt Sophie, and it was not long before we all knew that Father had been "sweet on Henrietta," as Aunt Sophie put it, long before he and Mother had met. But it was not Mother who had taken him from her. That was still another story, which Aunt Sophie let slip under Emily's skillful questioning, and involved another villager, Ann Byersford by name, to whom our susceptible young Father had paid his respects at the same time he was supposed to be courting Henrietta. It had made quite a stir in the village, Aunt Sophie told us, when Mother, fresh from a girls' boarding school in the States, had appeared on the scene and completely captivated him.

That was the story of Henrietta, though good old Aunt Sophie took pains to tell us earnestly that Father's real love had been Mother—he was merely courteous to the other young ladies, as any well-bred young man would have been. That we must fully understand.

However, all the explanations in the world could not erase from our minds the fact that Father's one-time sweetheart was about to be our guest, and by Mother's invitation.

Of course, among ourselves we speculated about her, wondered what she would be like, whether she would still be beautiful—for naturally she had been beautiful or Father would never have smiled on her—and so on and on, until we had worked ourselves up to such a pitch of excitement that we could scarcely pursue the everyday routine of our lives.

But what disappointment was ours when finally she arrived! I shall never forget it. Mother and Emily met her at the station, and we younger children gathered at the parlor windows to catch the first glimpse of this romantic person. It seemed an age before the phaeton made its appearance, but at last Miss Henrietta Smythe was in our midst, and we were all being introduced and receiving tepid kisses on our cheeks.

Could it be possible that she had ever been beautiful—this faded, colorless little person, whose wispy hair and dim eyes and severely plain dress seemed to be of the one nondescript, drab color? She had a timid voice and an almost furtive manner; her hands trembled as she lifted a cup of tea to her lips, and she seemed very tired and worn. But we were willing to make allowances; the long journey, the excitement at being in her old love's home, emotion at meeting her rival again, might all have been somewhat upsetting, so we welcomed her with our usual boisterous enthusiasm and were soon helping unpack her bags, turning her stiffly lined dresses inside out before hanging them away, and otherwise making ourselves useful, or perhaps, from her point of view, officious.

There were many pleasant things about Miss Smythe, we discovered as we became better acquainted with her, but we could never quite reconcile ourselves to Aunt Sophie's story that Father had once been sweet on her, or that she had been sweet on him. Certainly she was not heartbroken over his jilting for she paid very little attention to him, preferring, it seemed, to sit with Mother and Aunt Sophie, discussing old times, old friends, old ways. I can hear her gentle voice even now, as she ended a sentence with a sigh and "Those were the days, Caroline, those were the days. The fruit grew like magic in our garden, and Ma and Pa were so kind and good to us children."

It seemed she was now quite alone in the world, and poor, but she brought us gifts, nevertheless—buttons, quaint, glowing, brilliant buttons cut from grand dresses worn in former, more affluent years, buttons which made us younger girls the envy of all the owners of button strings in our school. Another priceless gift she left with me was the art of making wax flowers. Now I could rival Miss Dexter, I fondly believed, as I molded a large and imposing basket of roses, lilies of the valley, and forget-me-nots, all sprinkled with oil of cloves, to present to Father on his birthday.

Emily and Maud she taught to make miser's purses, and she gradually recovered from her initial embarrassment and fright—caused, we learned later, by her having carried away with her the key of the hotel room in Cleveland where she had passed the night on her way to Chicago. When the key had been safely returned by Uncle George, she often became quite merry, even laughing a bit when someone referred to the old days or to Ann Byersford. Ann, it seemed, still lived in the old house and still gave parties as of yore, which naturally brought the conversation around to party fare and to the wonderful cakes the Smythes had regaled their guests with in those carefree days.

Kneaded cakes had been a feature of the old Smythe

home, and Miss Henrietta still made them on occasions, so nothing would do but she must make some for us. They were strange cakes, we thought, but very nice served piping hot with plenty of butter. They seemed to have no other name than just Kneaded Cakes, and were made in this way:

⟨⟩ KNEADED CAKES ⟨⟩

Three-fourths of a pound of currants were washed, dried and spread out on a towel to dry, while three cups of flour were sifted with salt (about ¾ teaspoonful) and two or three tablespoons of sugar. These ingredients were all mixed thoroughly, then just enough sweet cream was added to make a soft dough. Miss Henrietta kneaded the mass until it was light and bubbly, and rolled it out about one-fourth inch thick. Finally she cut it in small rounds with the top of a teacup and baked the cakes on a hot, greased griddle, turning them once, then splitting and buttering them. Anna, much interested in the process, thought they might have been baked in a hot oven, but Miss Henrietta, although she agreed with her, still clung to the griddle as her Ma had done.

After she had traveled on to the nephew in Kansas, we often had Kneaded Cakes for tea, in memory of Miss Henrietta, though we could never have forgotten her, even if she had left behind her no mementos in the shape of button strings, miser's purses, and wax flowers.

Perhaps I am wrong in including Ellen Foster in this galaxy of Father's lady friends, for she was his relative, a second or third cousin several times removed, to be sure, but still of his tribe and regarded as a member of the family by all in our household. But that she admired him with a little more than a cousinly admiration could not be denied. At all events, Ellen never took the trouble to deny it. Father was her ideal, the standard in appearance, knowledge of the world, and wit, by which all other men of her acquaintance were judged.

Ellen had arrived in America shortly after Father and Mother were married, and her first home had been with them. She was elegantly educated, warm-hearted and very refined—so refined, as a matter of fact, that at her first introduction to corn on the cob, she wore white kid gloves while eating it. But that was long, long before my time, though the performance still remained fresh in Father's memory, and he never lost an opportunity to poke fun at her about it. It was one of those perennial family jokes we all enjoyed.

Ellen was now governess in a Very Rich family, and this, to us children, set her quite apart from ordinary folks. We adored her stories of the Very Rich children under her care, of their travels, their lessons, and their fine clothes; even their attacks of measles and chicken pox took on a certain glamour as Ellen recounted them. Their mother, according to the general opinion in our household, was frivolous; Ellen, it is true, was very loyal but now and then during the course of her conversation, bits of information would slip out which Aunt Sophie, and even Mother, declared could have no other significance—Mrs. Carson was evidently frivolous. Breakfast in bed, dinner at eight, silk stockings every day—of course she was frivolous!

Even so, Mrs. Carson was devoted to Ellen and chose her for a companion on thrilling journeys to Florida and other faraway places, from which points would come many strange and delightful gifts all addressed to Father in Ellen's dashing handwriting. An orchid for Mother's little conservatory; mysterious pink-lined shells with the sound of the sea still imprisoned within them—what an air of culture and elegance those shells lent to the white marble mantle in our front parlor—; little dried starfish; moss that floated rootless but living from the Florida trees, so Ellen

93

wrote; and pressed flowers. These were just a few of the fascinating souvenirs we were constantly receiving whenever Ellen traveled with the frivolous Mrs. Carson and her frivolous children, Jane and Georgie, who composed the Very Rich family.

And what presents she bestowed upon us all at Christmastime! I recall an imposing rose silk pin-cushion covered with bands of real lace joined with elaborately puffed footing. A deep ruffle of lace-edged footing spread itself bouffantly all round the edge of the cushion and was held in place at the corners with tassels of glass beads. Altogether too exciting and fine a pincushion for my mother's unimaginative bureau so it was wrapped carefully in an old linen pillow slip and laid away for festive occasions. But alas! the mice found its bran stuffing so alluring that they chewed the beautiful cushion almost into ribbons in their frenzy to get to it, and even after Miss Dexter had managed to repair it, the rose silk cushion could make its appearance only in a dimly lighted room.

Cousin Ellen brought us delicious tastes now and then when the Carsons had a party—Italian Creams, made by their expensive cook, to whom the Very Rich Mrs. Carson paid, so Ellen told us almost in a whisper, all of twenty dollars a week. Sometimes the elaborate dishes were accompanied by directions for their making, all meticulously written out by that same prized cook, but unfortunately calling for unheard-of ingredients, which made them impractical for our simple everyday household.

But her cakes were different, or perhaps Ellen only brought us the simpler sort that Jane and Georgie might have eaten at their early supper. However that may be, we thought them delicious. There was one that we especially liked and that Ellen liked to make for us on her free afternoons. "Ellen's Jelly Cake," we called it, and it went in this way:

⟨⟩ JELLY CAKE ⟨⟩

3 eggs	1 teaspoon baking powder
1 cup granulated sugar	¼ teaspoon salt
4 tablespoons orange juice or	½ teaspoon lemon extract
water	2 tablespoons hot melted
1 cup flour	butter

The eggs were beaten to a light, bubbly foam, the sugar and extract added, and the beating continued until the mixture was like a pale yellow batter. Then the liquid—orange juice preferably, but water or some other fruit juice if Ellen could not manage the oranges—was whipped in. The flour was sifted twice, the last time with the salt and baking powder, then tossed into the egg and sugar mixture by tablespoonfuls. The butter, hot almost to sizzling, was folded in just before the batter was put in the pans. As to the latter, they were the most interesting part of the whole performance. Shallow, shallow, round pans they were. Ellen buttered at least five, sometimes even six or seven of them, carefully dusted them with flour, and spread her cake batter into them, as thin as paper. In a moderate oven, say 350° according to modern standards, the cakes would bake in ten to twelve minutes, rising just enough to give them a delicate, light texture with a pale crust.

While the cakes were in the oven, Ellen beat one or two glasses of tart jelly to a paste, ready to spread between the cakes while they were piping hot. When all the thin layers had been piled one on top of the other, with layers of red jelly between them, the cake looked very large and luscious, and Ellen added to its tempting appearance by coating it all over with an orange or lemon-flavored icing. Sometimes the icing was also red. Ellen accomplished this by beating powdered sugar into the jelly. We thought Ellen's Jelly Cake decidedly stylish.

However, Father preferred a certain currant caraway

bun which reminded him of the old days in Ireland, when he and Ellen, as children, had eaten the cake fresh from the oven with cups of very strong tea, diluted for their drinking with plenty of milk. Ellen's currant buns were more to our liking than Henrietta Smythe's, except for the caraway seeds, which Father loved but which we cordially disliked. Fortunately, Ellen could make the currant buns, with one hand tied," as she said, they were so easy.

Currant Buns

2 cups flour	½ teaspoon salt
3 teaspoons baking powder (Ellen's mother had used soda and cream of tartar)	4 tablespoons sugar
	¾ cup milk
	1 cup currants
½ cup lard and butter mixed	1 teaspoon caraway seeds
	1 egg

The flour, baking powder, salt, and sugar were whisked through the sieve, and the shortening rubbed in well. The egg beaten, milk added to it, and the currants washed, dried in a clean towel, were stirred in with the seeds as a finishing touch. The dough was soft, sometimes almost too soft, and when that happened Ellen whisked in a spoonful or two more of flour. Then she broke off small pieces of the dough rolled them into balls, set them in a greased pan, brushed them over with a little milk and egg reserved from the mixing for this purpose, strewed a very little sugar over them, and baked them in a hot oven. Sometimes we split and buttered them while hot, but they were almost as good without this extra touch.

Other Kitchens, Other Cakes

I MUST HAVE BEEN a greedy youngster, I fear, for my happiest recollections of those old days in Chicago seem to center around cooking and baking, licking pans and spoons, poring over cookery books and trying out all the most elaborate concoctions I could find, for my own and my father's delectation.

Father was always cheerfully co-operative on those occasions, but I hate to think of all the queer mixtures he managed to make away with when I was seized with a culinary fervor. I liked my own cooking no matter what its results, and Father gallantly shared my liking, or professed to do so.

Even the old friends whom I remember most clearly seem to have been those at whose table I ate my fill of something that appealed to my adolescent appetite. Yes, I must have been a greedy young person.

But the cakes on the supper tables, or the cookies which, in the homes of our good friends, came in on thin silver plates, with tea, were not the sole attraction visiting held for me, though they did have their allure, I admit.

Because our family was so large and our household so merry and busy, we children did not go from home very often. Occasionally, however, Mother would be invited, in the hospitable fashion of the eighties, to spend the day with this old schoolmate or that friend, and sometimes the invitation would include the children—not all of them, of course, but which or how many, was left to her own discretion. These events were always gala occasions for the fortunate one chosen to accompany her, as almost every one of Mother's friends had something of deep interest in her house, something that made a whole day spent there one to be long remembered.

There was Mrs. McAlister, a tall, very thin, brittle sort of person, with piercing black eyes and a dewlap under her chin. The McAlisters lived in a large brown house way out on the north shore of Lake Michigan. A fascinating garden, where life-sized iron deer and gay little wooden gnomes made merry in their quiet way under the trees, surrounded the house, and a green swing on springs, the first one of its kind we had ever seen, occupied the center of the grass plot. Close by the kitchen door was the cistern, half sunken in the ground, which supplied the McAlister family with water.

The cistern, for all its pretty covering of green moss, constituted a very disagreeable feature, the only disagreeable feature, I am sure, of our visits to Mrs. McAlister. Cistern water as a beverage we cordially detested, but as Mr. and Mrs. McAlister drank it always and seemed to think very well of it, we could do the same or parch with thirst, for nothing else was offered. So when Mother received her semiannual invitation to spend the day and bring one of the girls with her, my sisters were always very, very busy, or they had sore throats, or something else would interfere with their going, and I would be led to the sacrifice, fortified with many glasses of pure, clear water from Lake Michigan before starting out, and wearing Emily's red sash by way of recompense.

In the McAlister home was a collection of old books which had belonged to the McAlister children, and once I had paid my respects to Mrs. McAlister, I was free to browse among them to my heart's content. I might even take them to the garden, where, seated grandly on the back of an iron deer or lolling deliciously in the swing, I could read for hours, uninterruptedly.

My favorite volume was the *Arabian Nights' Entertainments*. Old, torn, dog-eared, pages missing, I loved it, and I think I must have read it through from cover to cover more than once on those occasions when we spent the day with Mrs. McAlister. Its romance and adventure charmed me, but I did not read it solely on that account. It was the mouth-watering descriptions of cream cakes, cucumbers stuffed with pearls, lamb cooked with pistachio nuts, pomegranate seeds, and feastings of great magnificence, that fascinated me. But the stories cast their spell over me too, and I would dream the morning away until the call to dinner brought me back to the unpleasant realism of life, beginning with the McAlisters' drinking water.

Mrs. McAlister's table always groaned with good things, and although she herself ate little being afflicted with stomach trouble (due, Uncle George claimed, to drinking rain water), she proudly upheld the traditions of her family, which descended from a Pennsylvania Dutch ancestor.

As I took my seat Lena would very likely be in the act of pouring the water from the large clear glass pitcher, with its raised decorations of pears and strawberries, into glasses that matched it exactly. Pale yellow was the water, like very weak lemonade, tepid, flat, and altogether calculated to spoil any unaccustomed appetite but my own. Mother was given her choice of tea or coffee, and so escaped the distasteful beverage. No substitute was offered me but I contrived to get along quite well, little glutton that I was, by taking large mouthfuls of the very good food, with very small sips of the warmish cistern water to wash them down.

I recall but a few of the strange dishes we ate at Mrs. McAlister's—dishes which Mr. Mac and the boys and I devoured with keen appreciation. I know there were noodles cooked in every conceivable manner, sometimes a luscious dish of ham cooked with dried apples, but my favorite was stewed chicken with potato dumplings, something totally unfamiliar to me. Mother's dumplings were light, golden, fluffy things cooked in gravy, or they were dessert dumplings made with fruit, and served with our pet hard sauce.

Lena's potato dumplings were the most savory things imaginable. They were flavored with onion, I think. After simmering them in the rich chicken broth Lena browned them in plenty of butter and surrounded them with little cubes of bread which were also browned to a delectable nut shade in the butter.

Lena often gave us Dutch apple pies and cheese custards, which to my notion compared very favorably with the toothsome things I had read of and hankered for in the *Arabian Nights' Entertainments*, but her Funnel Cakes were the most diverting of all the good things she made.

Funnel Cakes were usually served hot, on those occasions when spending the day meant that Father would come for supper and a game of whist, and he and Mother and I would drive home in the lovely summer night. Lena made the Funnel Cakes in the late afternoon and usually would invite me into her kitchen for a chat, for she loved to hear about Anna and Emil and all the affairs at our home. Hired girls in those days felt themselves members of the family, very necessary members, too, and took a lively interest in everything that concerned their folks. So Lena would make the Funnel Cakes at the last possible moment before supper, with me as a very inquisitive onlooker.

⌒ FUNNEL CAKES ⌒

First she would put a pint of milk over the fire, and when it had just reached the boiling point she would set it aside to cool a bit, meantime beating one or two eggs to a froth and sifting a pint and a half of flour with half a teaspoonful each of soda and salt and a tablespoonful of sugar. Then she would stir the flour into the lukewarm milk, add the beaten eggs, and turn the well-beaten batter into a large funnel. The interesting part came next. Holding her finger over the opening in the funnel, she would wave it round and round over hot fat, allowing just enough of the batter to escape to make all sorts of interesting shapes, figure eights, rings, pretzels, and other forms as her fancy dictated. As the cakes puffed up and cooked, they came to the surface of the fat and were turned over, and when they were deliciously browned on both sides, Lena would skim them out with with a fork, drain them on brown paper for a moment then dash to the table with them. We ate Lena's incomparable Funnel Cakes with maple sirup or homemade apple butter, and, my, but they were good!

After supper I returned to the kitchen, where I wiped the dishes for Lena and ate the last remaining Funnel Cakes, because, as she remarked, they would be no good at all the next day, and it would favor her greatly if I would help her to get rid of them. And of course I was always glad to do her any favor so delightful as eating her good cakes.

Kate McAlister, only daughter of the house of McAlister, was my idea of all that a grand lady should be, stately handsome, eyes burning black, hair like jet, worn in a large roll wrapped round her head, as she would have worn a coronet. Lena told me privately that Kate's hair, when it was let down, reached to her knees, and that it was "rope thick." Kate was married to a very prosperous husband, and lived in a fine house on the fashionable North Side. She wore elegant clothes, hats with coque plumes that swept splendidly over her shoulder, gloves of brightest red, green, or purple kid, high shoes with tasseled laces, heavy gold bracelets, and a watch chain, which, after circling her throat mant times, draped itself over her bosom, where a rich gold pin set with a diamond caught it and her dazzling watch securely.

Yes, Kate McAlister was a very splendid person, but not too elegant frequently to enjoy spending an easygoing, unexciting day in our household. When she had shed the stylish hat stretched the vivid kid gloves by blowing deep breaths into them, and laid them away with the gold bracelets and the watch and chain, she would take a piece of embroidery, that year after year never seemed to be any nearer completion, from her chatelaine bag, and settle herself for a carefree day.

Occasionally Father and Mother and my older sisters were invited to a euchre party at Kate's, and it was at one of these gatherings that we acquired the receipt for a new and very stylish cake. White Mountain Cake they called it. Kate, who liked to be first in everything, even to the refreshments for her parties, had paid a fabulous sum for this receipt, so they said, but she willingly gave it to Mother under the seal of strict secrecy. Thereafter, Mother kept Kate's calling card, with the receipt scrawled over it, under lock and key, and not even Anna was permitted to enter the kitchen while White Mountain Cake was in the process of making.

However, as the cake grew more and more famous, it became impossible to keep the rules for its making a secret, so it passed from one housewife to another, in the way all good receipts travel, until it probably went halfway round the world. Here it is, just as my mother set it down in her book of very special receipts.

ᗑ WHITE MOUNTAIN CAKE ᗒ

"Take ¾ cup of butter and beat until like whipped cream, add 2 cups of sifted fine sugar, and beat again to a foam. Add 1 teaspoon of vanilla (or almond in less quantity). Sift 3 cups of flour with the risings, which may be ¾ teaspoon cream of tartar and ½ teaspoon of soda, or 3 small spoonfuls of baking powder, as you please, and add this to the creamed butter and sugar a little at a time, alternating with a cup of sweet milk. Now, having beat the whites of six eggs to a stiff but not dry state, fold them delicately into the batter, which should not be stirred or beaten too much. Bake this batter in four layer tins about eight inches in diameter, taking care that the cakes do not become brown; they should be of a pale tan tint.

"*Icing and filling for this cake*: Sift twice 1½ cups fine granulated sugar and add a pinch of cream of tartar, with ¼ cup water; put over the fire to boil, with no stirring after the boiling begins. Try the sirup in a little cold water, and when it makes a soft ball pour it over the stiffly beaten whites of two eggs. Continue beating while pouring, and afterward until the icing cools and stiffens somewhat. Flavor as you flavored the cake, but very delicately, spread over each layer of cake, and sprinkle liberally with coconut. Put together in a high tiered cake, ice the top and sides, and strew coconut over the entire cake. A very handsome ornament and a tasty sweet."

Although White Mountain Cake was imposing and delicious, there was another McAlister cake that to us younger children was even more alluring and wonderful. We discovered it at the John McAlisters one enchanting day when we were asked for dinner. The John McAlisters were not fashionable people, though they lived in a nice house in a section of the South Side considered very genteel. John was Kate's brother and the oldest son of Mr. and

103

VICTORIAN CAKES

Mrs. McAlister. John's wife was a busy, comfortable little woman, simple in her ways, but striving as best she could to keep up with sister Kate. Nettie, her own sister lived with her, and together the two women kept the house and the two little McAlister daughters shining and spotless. Aunt Sophie thought it rather a shame that poor Nettie had no time nor opportunity to catch herself a beau, but Nettie seemed happy and contented, and they were all very jolly and pleasant.

We always loved to go to the John McAlisters. The dinner was bound to be a specially grand one, for Nettie, who loved to cook, was on her mettle when Mother was a guest. Then, too, the little McAlister girls went to dancing school, which set them very high in our estimation. Moreover, they obligingly taught us the new steps, which we practiced sedulously at home after lessons were studied in the evenings, with Mother to coach us and Uncle George taking us in turn through the mazes of the waltz and polka, Aunt Sophie humming and keeping time with her head. Such delight! Father did not believe in dancing, but usually the evening would end with a grand reel or quadrille, the whole family skipping about and bowing to partners while benign old Aunt Sophie would play "The Irish Washerwoman" or "Charlie Is My Darling" on the piano with one finger.

I shall always remember the day Nettie surprised us with her entrancing Walnut-Apple Dessert Cake. It was an unforgettable day. Kitty and I had new dresses to wear, embroidered white linen with the fringed Roman sashes Cousin Ellen had sent us from Europe; our hair, dampened and tightly plaited the night before, was combed out in a mass of frizzes that hung to our waists, and tied round our heads were real silk ribbons that matched the sashes, instead of the ugly tan "lutestring" kind we usually wore on our taffy-colored braids. That was enough to make any day perfect. Aunt Sophie was invited, too—another cause for rejoicing; and we cheerfully squeezed ourselves into the phaeton, Mother and Aunt Sophie with Emily, who drove, on the none too wide seat, Kitty and I on small hassocks on the floor. I don't think we uttered one word of complaint through the long three hours' drive, so happy were we.

But the cake, the marvelous Walnut-Apple Dessert Cake that Nettie made for us that memorable day! There it was, reposing on a high glass cake stand in the center of the lavishly spread table, when we sat ourselves down to the one o'clock dinner. An ethereal cake, so light, so feathery, so delicate that it was impossible to do anything with it but put it slowly and prayerfully in one's appreciative mouth, a very little at a time to make it last longer, and then sit with closed, ecstatic eyes while it slid down one's greedy but delighted throat.

All through the afternoon while we youngsters danced and capered, the remains of that gorgeous cake stood on the sideboard. I wondered about it, who would eat it, and when and where; and I recall how relieved I felt when, just before we left for our long journey home, Mrs. McAlister cut it into four pieces and gave it to us children.

Of course we carried the receipt for the sumptuous dessert home with us. I have it still in my old diary. Spongecake of a very light, delicate quality, baked in two rather deep, square layer-cake pans, formed its foundation. The cakes, while still slightly warm, were put together with a delicious, pale-tinted applesauce, which was first pressed through a very fine strainer, sweetened, chilled, blended with an equal amount of stiffly whipped cream, and embellished by the addition of a handful of finely chopped English walnut meats. With this filling, almost an inch high, between the cakes, the result was something quite wonderful to my young, desirous eyes. But that was not all, by any means. Sweetened whipped cream flavored ever so faintly with grated lemon rind and enriched by more chopped nuts was piled in mountainous heaps over the top of the cake, and halved nut meats, arranged over the whole, added their luscious charm. The cake was served in generous squares with cups of whipped-cream-topped chocolate to wash it down. Is it any wonder my memory serves me so well?

It was always a red letter day for me when I went visiting with Mother, but there were some friends of my very own with whom I loved to spend an afternoon, untrammeled by any family restrictions. The Warners I particularly adored.

Mr. and Mrs. Warner were an intellectual, elderly couple with minds as guileless and naive as children's. They were without kith or kin, and lived a sort of Arcadian existence in an enchanting, shabby house, filled to overflowing with books, which they were forever reading and discussing. Food, to them, was something that required consideration, of course, but not too much. There were "other things of so much greater importance in life than mere eating and drinking, my dear."

Beside their treasured books, they had an equally treasured garden and a tiny conservatory wherein strange plants grew and flourished and put forth exotic blooms. Mrs. Warner talked to her flowers as though they were human beings, coaxing, reprimanding, praising them, as she snipped off faded leaves, gave them their daily drink of water and stirred the soil about them as one would shake up a baby's pillow. The garden was Mr. Warner's cherished child. I used to think he talked to his trees and shrubs as Mrs. Warner did to her flowers, but I never quite caught him doing it.

Each summer Mrs. Warner would give a party to which the whole neighborhood was invited. Only little store cookies very dry and stale, with weak lemonade, were offered in the way of refreshment, but there was always a feast of good talk—and, too, there was the night-blooming cereus, the chief actor at the party. I remember how we all sat around the library watching the uncanny plant slowly unfolding its blossom, and how many of the older folks spoke in hushed voices, just as they had at Mr. Anderson's funeral. It was usually twelve o'clock before the proud flower reached its full beauty, but I think everyone felt amply repaid for the long wait. I know I returned home to my bed feeling that I had witnessed a miracle.

Sometimes when I went calling on the Warners, Mrs. Warner, who was delicate and slightly lame, would ask me to go on delightful errands for her, carrying flowers to friends who were ill, or celebrating birthdays or some other happy anniversary. Now and then I carried joyous bouquets to new babies. I specially loved these occasions, for Mrs. Warner made these nosegays so enchanting—a calla lily filled with sweet-scented garden pinks and Johnny-jump-ups, or tiny pink rosebuds wreathed with candytuft and forget-me-nots. It was a great honor, I thought, to be the bearer of such exquisite offerings.

Mr. Warner was tall, dignified, studious, and very patient, particularly with his frail wife. His dark hair, frosted over with gray crinkled thickly over his head, and his serious eyes could twinkle and gleam merrily on occasion. How well I recollect that kind old neighbor who was never too busy or too much in the clouds to help me with a problem or suggest a topic for a composition. I loved to sit in his library, still as a mouse, while he read Emerson or Thoreau to me. Whether I understood all their philosophy or not, I thrilled at the sound of Mr. Warner's voice. To be invited to stay for dinner or supper at the Warner's sent me into the seventh heaven of bliss, not because of my usual greedy anticipations, but because the conversation at their table was always so fascinating, even though very often over my head.

As to the menu, it might be colorless and nondescript—that was to be expected at the Warners, where eating to live, as they frequently remarked, was far more important than living to eat—but the dessert was irresistible, though it seldom varied. Year in and year out, in all seasons, the Warners ate shortcake. Mr. Warner loved short-cake, and Mrs. Warner loved to make it for him— strawberry, raspberry, peach, blackberry, not to mention early rhubarb and June apples—all through the summer they reveled in shortcake and then prolonged the season with grapes or pears. When these were gone, they carried right on through the winter with the dried fruits, and winter applesauce, not forgetting cranberry and orange shortcake. The latter Mr. Warner put just second to strawberry. Pineapple and bananas were new and strange to us in the eighties, or I am sure Mrs. Warner would have turned them into shortcakes along with the other fruits, and although she detested cooking and cared not a great deal for eating, Mrs. Warner's shortcakes were masterpieces. Probably much practice had made her perfect. At all events, shortcake was the favorite, almost the only, dessert ever served in their household. I remember once when I was their guest, Mrs. Warner decided to vary the usual order of things and even today I recall Mr. Warner's pained face when ice cream made its appearance.

"Why, Susie," he exclaimed petulantly, like a disappointed child. "I thought today would be a shortcake day."

"We've had shortcake every day for goodness knows how long," Mrs. Warner answered, "and I felt I wanted a change. I'm sorry, Henry."

"Well, never mind, Susie, you were raised a pet and I expect I must go on spoiling you," submissively replied her husband. But child though I was, I noticed that when

Susie found a piece of yesterday's shortcake and set it before him, his face lighted up as at the sight of a long-vanished friend.

"Susie's Maple Shortcake" was one of Mr. Warner's early spring delights. I loved it too, and Mrs. Warner gave it to him frequently. It was a rich biscuit dough, in which cream took the place of milk, rolled half an inch thick and placed in two layers in a well-buttered dripping pan, dots of butter being placed between the layers. When it was baked, it was split and buttered with an unstinting hand, then sprinkled thickly with shaved maple sugar. The top layer was turned baked side down, and well buttered and masked with rich, damp, maple sugar. We ate it with cream which now seems to me rather overdoing a good thing, but in my girlhood, Susie's Maple Shortcake, smothered in cream and eaten in company with Mr. Warner, spelled perfection.

When the big cherry tree in the Warner garden was full of dead-ripe, luscious fruit, Mr. Warner demanded shortcake for breakfast. I can vouch for its deliciousness, as there was usually a piece saved for me. The snappy tartness of the cherries and the tempting lightness of the cake formed a combination that ravished my rapacious palate. Mrs. Warner made the cake with buttermilk, rich with little particles of butter floating about on its surface, or if that was not forthcoming, she used sour cream, stirring a scant teaspoon of soda into a pint and beating until foamy and singing. Then she stirred in two tablespoons of sugar, a good pinch of salt, and enough flour to make a soft dough, which she spread in two well-buttered tins and baked in a hot oven.

But the Cherry Shortcake really began the afternoon before, when Mr. Warner picked the fruit, discarding all but the most perfect, looked it over carefully, and washed it at the pump. Then he and Mrs. Warner would sit in a shady spot on the back porch and pit the cherries. This was an interesting occupation to me, for she always recited some long poem during the pitting operation. I learned Thanatopsis by heart over pans of red, ripe cherries one summer. When the fruit was pitted, it was covered generously with granulated sugar, stirred well, and set in a cool place overnight. When the cakes were baked and nicely browned, Mrs. Warner would split and butter them, and spread the rich, sugared cherries between the layers and over the top. Certainly it was good, a perfect breakfast dish, and one did not need a down-East palate like Mr. Warner's to appreciate it.

Once or twice every summer, during the long vacations, we younger children spent the day with Grandma Whitney. Father would bring us into the city in the old Democrat wagon on his morning trip to his office and call for us on his homeward way in the late afternoon. He would also, often much against his will bring our dolls and their entire wardrobes, our button strings, the fancy work we might be engaged upon, and anything else we especially wanted to show Grandma—not our own grandmother, to be sure, nor was she the grandmother of anyone in the world. Nevertheless, she was "Grandma" Whitney to countless numbers of people, old and young, big and little, who loved her devotedly.

Grandma Whitney would have been very much disappointed had we left our treasures at home, for she knew every member of the doll family by name, and loved them all almost as much as we did. She would sit by the hour examining our button strings and listening to our tales of special new additions to our collections; very likely she would have sun-dry additions to make herself. She would play our games with real spirit, and help us over hard places in our needlework or crocheting, thoroughly enjoying herself all through the long day.

Grandma was a hale and hearty old lady with several chins, beady brown eyes that were never anything but kind, and a sweet buttonhole mouth which distributed kisses to us and to our doll children quite impartially.

Such a good time as we had at her tiny home!—not alone because of her merry ways and honest affection, but because of Blackberry Cake. Blackberry Cake would be served hot with plenty of cream or a rich lemon sauce for dinner, and in the afternoon, before Father called for us, Grandma's nice old hired girl, Freda, would bring in slices of the cold cake and a pitcher of cool homemade root beer to regale us and send us on our way with no regrets. We relished that unusual attention almost more than any of the day's joys. When I grew older Freda taught me how to make the cake myself, and I was a proud girl the first time my cake was served at Grandma's dinner table. I have made it many times since, and always I am reminded of the quaint old parlor with the clove apple on the whatnot, and the framed wreath made of hair flowers which hung on the wall, and I can almost see Grandma herself kissing the dolls goodby, as Father and Emil and the Democrat wagon drove up to the curb. Here is old Freda's receipt:

⌒ BLACKBERRY CAKE ⌒

½ cup butter	½ teaspoon mixed cinnamon
1 cup sugar	and nutmeg
3 eggs	3 teaspoons baking powder
2 cups flour	Pinch of salt
½ cup milk	2 cups blackberries

Freda creamed the butter and sugar together in the usual way, whipped in the beaten yolks of the eggs, sifted flour, baking powder, salt, and spices together and added them alternately with the milk. Then she folded the whites of the eggs, already beaten to a stiff foam, and finally and very gently turned in the blackberries, which, she was care-

111

ful to explain, should be ripe but not soft, and well dusted with flour. The idea was, she said, not to let the berries break, but to keep them as nearly whole as possible until the cake was finished. She baked it in a shallow loaf-cake pan for half an hour or a little longer and iced it with a brown-sugar frosting that we dearly loved.

When I had learned to make it quite perfectly at Grandma's, I tried it at home as a surprise for my father, and thereafter he demanded it once every week as long as blackberries lasted. When the fresh berry season had ended, I used blackberry jam and found I had an entirely new and different kind of cake. Of course I had to make one for Grandma and Freda, and that meant another joyous visit.

Not far from Grandma Whitney's little red brick house was the more pretentious home of her daughter, Mrs. James Hardy. Mrs. Hardy was one of my mother's oldest and best-loved friends. In fact, they had both attended Miss Apple's Finishing School for Young Ladies, and the friendship begun in their girlhood had never cooled or wavered. We children would listen avidly when they discussed their old boarding-school days. We loved to hear the cruel tales of loaves so thinly sliced and so meagerly spread that our naughty mother was once punished for turning her slice over and over, to see, as she explained, "on which side her bread was buttered." We adored stories of the stern teacher who frowned upon innocent handkerchief flirtations with charming cadets in a near-by military academy, and who administered raps on the knuckles of the offenders; and we thrilled when they spoke of the dancing master who came once a week to teach the young ladies grace and deportment, and with whom most of the girls were violently in love. It was good fun, we thought, when Mother and Mrs. Hardy talked, and more fun when they forgot their age and dignified stations in life, and to our secret amusement—for we considered them very old ladies—began humming and curtsying and bowing to each other in the quaint figures of the minuet, as taught by their romantic young dancing master. When we danced, we waltzed, or schottisched, or did that disgracefully modern racket. A day at Mrs. Hardy's was always grand fun!

A classic in both Mrs. Hardy's home and our own was her famous Pork Cake, a dark, rich concoction which Mother often made for Thanksgiving, and which was never absent from Mrs. Hardy's table, winter or summer, when her genial, kindly husband was at home. Captain Jamie, as everyone called him, was a well-to-do owner and operator of a Great Lakes steamer. He was short, chubby, and cherubic of face, with a gray curl on the top of his head like that of a little boy still in dresses, and a funny little paintbrush beard on his chin. His big, hearty voice used to boom through the house like a foghorn, and at the sound everyone would perk up and begin immediately to have a good time. Captain Hardy thought most of the modern cakes newfangled and fussy, but vowed he could eat his weight in Pork Cake, and he probably did many times over in the course of his lifetime.

Mrs. Hardy's brother Henry, a tall, lanky man who had been told he resembled Abraham Lincoln, had once presented his sister with a very elegant cake basket, and even today when I think of Pork Cake, I always picture it cut in large man-sized wedges, piled high in that handsome basket, Henry's wonderful gift.

Mrs. Hardy, or Hulda, her hired girl, started the Pork Cake on its way the night before the Captain's return from a voyage, when they prepared the fruit and put half a pound of fat salt pork cut in small pieces, to freshen in cold water. In the morning they drained the pork well, chopped it very fine, and then—but here is Mrs. Hardy's very own receipt:

VICTORIAN CAKES

⟨⟩ PORK CAKE ⟨⟩

½ pound fat salt pork
1 cup boiling water
1 cup brown sugar
1 cup molasses
½ teaspoon soda
1 wineglass sherry or brandy
Cinnamon, cloves, nutmeg
  as desired
½ pound dates

½ pound raisins
½ pound hickory nut meats
½ pound dried apricots or
  prunes
1 cup sweetened applesauce
¼ cup shaved citron
¼ cup mixed candied
  orange and lemon peel
Flour to make a stiff batter

After the pork was chopped, the boiling water was poured over it, the sugar, soda and molasses added, then the raisins and nut meats coarsely chopped. The apricots or prunes, steamed slightly and delicately sliced, were stirred in also; and the applesauce, spices, and wine or brandy were turned in, and all beaten well. Finally the flour, sifted twice, was slowly mixed with the other ingredients, always with care that not too much was used, for that would make the cake hard and stiff. When the batter was just right, it was stirred vigorously until the fruits were well distributed and the whole thing a deliciously spicy mass; then it was baked in a large buttered tube pan, or in two smaller pans, in a very, very careful oven. Mrs. Hardy's receipt made a large cake that required at least three hours' baking in a very moderate oven. When Mother made Pork Cake she used to brush it with brandy when it was taken, hot and spicy, from the oven, and after it had cooled, she wrapped it in paper, then in a clean cloth, and tucked it away in her stone crock with an apple beside it. She never iced it, chiefly, I think, because Captain Hardy scorned icing and Mrs. Hardy's receipt called for no such embellishment. But when Emily and Maud became the family cake makers, Pork Cake usually made its appearance gaily dressed in a thick white frosting flavored with orange, lemon or sherry, and further beautified with halved nut meats or bits of citron. It was a remarkable cake, with or without this adornment, and one Father dearly loved.

"No one," exclaimed Aunt Sophie, "no one in the world would ever have believed that Mrs. Serenus Hale could so much as peel a potato, much less cook it, but look at that cake! Will wonders never cease?"

The cake we were bidden to gaze upon was a noble Hickory Nut Loaf, smooth, shining, and thickly strewn with luscious nut meats. It stood there in the very center of the dining-room table where Mrs. Hale had placed it, with Mrs. Hale herself, flushed, excited, and triumphant, stationed close by, as though to guard the masterpiece she had created, the rest of us hanging about wondering when the delectable thing was to be cut, and waiting, tongues literally hanging out, for our share of it. It seemed, however, that we were to be doomed to disappointment. The entire cake was to be wrapped most carefully and carried via our phaeton, with Emily driving, to Mrs. Hale's home, for Mr. Serenus Hale's birthday party.

"But I'll come back another day and make one just for you," she remarked as she tucked herself into the phaeton and took the precious package on her knees. "Don't forget, specially you, Aunt Sophie—I'll show you how well I can cook."

"Poor little sprite," mumbled our old auntie as she waved goodby, "never has had half a chance in those cooped-up rooms of hers."

Which was probably true, for the Hales did "light housekeeping," a phrase just coming in to fashion and sounding most fascinating to us young folks. Serenus Hale was an artist, and they lived in what Uncle George and Aunt Sophie considered an almost disreputable fashion in his studio. All the evidences of housekeeping and cooking were cleverly disguised in some artistic way; the coal hod wore a skirt of embroidered velvet; the diminutive dishpan was masked through the day with a covering of gaily painted pasteboard, and held a rubber plant; the few necessary cups, plates, saucepans, and skillets were ranged on shelves behind curtains of satin on which lilies worked in tinsel thread grew as naturally as in life. The cooking was all done over a gas jet on which at mealtime a special burner was placed. It must have been fun, we young folks thought, playing at housekeeping in this way! Mrs. Hale was quite at home in this environment. So little and dainty she was, with ashy blonde hair, wide, light blue eyes, skin stretched almost too tightly over her face, tiny hands and feet—just a doll of a woman compared to our husky frames—but what made her so extremely fascinating to me were the spit curls all round her face. Those over her temples kept time as she ate, pulsating in and out with the regularity of clock work. It was most exciting to watch them.

We could never quite fit Mr. Hale into the light housekeeping picture he was so tall and stately. A sort of third or fourth cousin of Mother's, he felt that kinship excuse enough for bringing his fairy-like wife very frequently to Sunday night supper, and really, as Mother used to remark after they had gone their ways to call on some brother artist, for a little woman, Mrs. Hale had an excellent appetite; but perhaps that was noticeable merely because her spit curls made her operations in eating so marked. But Aunt Sophie and Father contended that both Mr. and Mrs. Hale were half starved. They used to press the cold meat and the buttered toast and cake and jam on them until we children, whiling away the time while waiting our turn at the crowded table by peeking through a crack in the door, used to fear there would be nothing left for us.

However, it was through Mrs. Hale that we discovered one of our most tempting, most popular cakes, the splendid Hickory Nut Loaf. She had a great desire to make this very cake for her husband's birthday she said, and as it would be impossible to attempt it over a gas ring, asked Mother to let her do it in our kitchen. Mother, of course, offered either to make him a cake herself, or to ask one of my sisters to do it, but Mrs. Hale preferred to have no hands touch the precious cake but her own, and Mother, with many misgivings, consented, and so tiny, helpless Mrs. Hale produced such a wonderful cake that it became a legend in our cake archives. And she kept her promise, and soon too; for one day she arrived with the hickory nuts all picked from their shells, the flour and sugar and butter measured out and tied in paper bags, even the eggs nestled snugly in the bottom of her chatelaine bag, without a single catastrophe, and here is her receipt for the fine Hickory Nut Loaf:

✑ HICKORY NUT LOAF ✑

1 cup butter	1 cup chopped hickory nut
2 cups sugar	meats
1 teaspoon lemon juice	2½ cups flour
4 eggs	½ teaspoon soda
¾ cup milk	Pinch of salt
1 cup chopped raisins	

It was fun to see little Mrs. Hale bustling about our great kitchen. Anna got her a footstool to stand on while she creamed the butter and sugar and added the lemon juice and beaten egg yolks at Mother's table. I sifted the flour, soda, and salt together for her, and Maud whipped the egg whites to a stiff froth. She added the raisins and nut meats to the egg and sugar mixture, then spooned the flour in alternately with the milk, folded in the egg whites and turned the batter into a tube pan, first rubbing it with softened butter and sprinkling it with flour. The baking required about an hour in a moderate oven, and while it was under way, Mrs. Hale surprised us by washing all the soiled bowls and spoons, thereby winning more laurels, this time from Anna. When the cake was finished it smelled so delicious we thought it would be a good plan to eat it at once, but Mrs. Hale insisted on icing it and arranging halved hickory nut meats all over it, exactly as she had dressed up Mr. Hale's birthday cake.

When we ate the cake that evening, everyone, even Aunt Sophie, had to admit that it was a truly wonderful cake, and that Mrs. Hale herself was a wonderful little person.

The Pickrell boys, Johnny, Cy, and Frank, lived with their parents Mr. and Mrs. Charles Pickrell, in a many-gabled house at the very end of our street. Mr. Pickrell did not go into the city in the mornings like Father and the other men in the neighborhood. He stayed at home and helped Mrs. Pickrell with the cooking and housework, but the boys, handsome young men, older than my sisters, but very attractive to them, nevertheless, were all in business and had to pass our home in the evenings as they walked from the end of the horsecar line to their own door.

My sisters, dressed and curled and perfumed, were usually in the garden or on the veranda at that time, and the Pickrell boys would bow gracefully, and even, if Father was not about, stop for a moment's chat, but they were never invited to come in—never!

Mr. Pickrell was a little man who had once upon a time had the misfortune to break his nose, which disfigured him somewhat, but seemed to endear him all the more to his wife. She was a gentle, slender person with lovely graying curls which she twirled about a stick each morning, clustering at each side of her face, a style passé even in the eighties, but very distinguished as Mrs. Pickrell wore it.

Every morning Mr. and Mrs. Pickrell would pass our house on their way to the lake shore, where they spent an hour or two walking up and down on the sands, picking up odd stones and pretty shells for their rockery, a minute mountain, trailing with vines and columbine, which they had built over an old barrel in their garden. Sometimes Kitty and I would be asked to join them and help pick up stones. Every unusual one would be greeted with delight. One discovery of my own, I particularly remember, glistened like diamonds, and was given a very conspicuous place in the rockery. It was always pointed out to visitors as Caroline's rock. Now and then little Charlie, their grandson from Buffalo, would visit them. With his golden mop of curly hair, his eyes merry and bright blue, and his little mouth the sweetest thing in the world to kiss, he always reminded me of the Cupid I had read of in Mr. Warner's library.

When Charlie was their guest Mrs. Pickrell would invite us to a tea party and we never failed to accept, though privately little Charlie seemed a mere baby to us who were now in the fourth or fifth grade. As befitted the occasion and the youth of the guest of honor, the refreshments were very simple—ginger cookies in the shapes of animals, birds, and fish, accompanied by mugs of weak cocoa. But we enjoyed going to Mrs. Pickrell's house, always so spotlessly clean and orderly, although she never seemed to do any sweeping or dusting, but was forever ironing the Pickrell boys' shirts, while Mr. Pickrell ironed the many, many handkerchiefs these same extravagant Pickrell boys seemed to require.

Mrs. Pickrell's ginger cookies were wonderful at any time, but at Christmas I think she surpassed even herself, or else we were so happy on that day that they tasted better. I can feel yet the thrill that seized me as, bundled up in scarfs with red crocheted hoods tied snugly under our chins, Kitty and I would fairly fly over the crisp snow on Christmas morning, bearing to Mr. and Mrs. Pickrell our gifts of mottoes worked on perforated cardboard, pen-wipers of scalloped circles of bright red flannel held together by steel buttons in the centers, or hair receivers crocheted and stretched over empty baking-powder cans. She would have our gifts ready for us, parcels of her famous gingerbread horses, stars, birds, even Christmas trees, all iced with a delicious, thick white icing and sprinkled with pink sugar or caraway comfits. They were so pretty we hated to break them, but such spiciness as they emitted proved too great a temptation, and so even before the hour in which we received them had passed, they were always devoured.

As I grew older I wanted to make gingerbread horses and stars myself, and Mrs. Pickrell obligingly gave me her receipt and helped me over any difficulties that beset me. It goes like this:

ᓚ GINGERBREAD COOKIES ᓚ

"The dough for making these little cakes is peculiar until you become familiar with it, then it is quite simple to make the cakes. Boil together for five minutes one cupful of dark molasses, 1 cup brown sugar, and 1 cup of shortening; add a teaspoon of soda, a pinch each of cinnamon, nutmeg, and ginger, and stir well. Remove from the fire and stir in as much sifted flour as the liquid can take care of, set the bowl in a pan of hot water, as the dough must be kept warm and pliable, otherwise it will soon become unmanageable. Take out a small portion and knead until it is like putty then roll very thin and cut into shapes. Bake in a moderate oven, always remembering that anything containing molasses will scorch quickly; then ice and decorate. When first baked, the cookies will be very hard, but if packed away in a closely covered tin box they will grow tender and crisp."

Mrs. Pickrell cut her cookies from patterns made by Mr. Pickrell, who seemed to enjoy the Christmas gingerbread making as much as she did. Together they made them by the hundreds, and I think every child of their acquaintance was made happy with a packet of the cakes tied round with bits of ribbon. But they didn't give them all away, for the Pickrell boys also loved them, and—this was a secret Mrs. Pickrell warned me not to tell my big sisters—they would have felt very downcast had they not found a good supply of them in their own stockings on Christmas morning.

The Round Lady

*A*NNA'S PLACE in our household was firmly establistablished. From Father down we all looked upon her as a member of the family, and a most important member at that. Never would we have been so cruel as to allude to her as a servant. Anna was our friend, who in return for a comfortable home and a few dollars in actual money each week, gave us loyal and faithful devotion. That she worked over the cookstove and sink, and scrubbed tables and floors in our kitchen, did not seem menial or ignoble to her nor to any of us. She was just Our Anna, and we children loved and respected her, and I am sure she had a warm affection for every one of us. Her admiration and regard for Mother were boundless, and as for Father, he was her ideal of all that was noble and splendid.

Father settled all difficulties that might arise in Anna's family, advised, counseled, berated, as the need might be; he was the last word in every discussion, and to the whole German settlement on Clybourne Avenue he was arbiter and referee. So Anna was glad and proud to work in our home; glad and proud to scour and polish until everything in the house shone; glad to peel vegetables and wash endless dishes; but especially glad and very proud to be asked to contribute one of her famous German cakes to our Sun-

123

day evening repasts, or at Christmastime to be entrusted with the huge task of cooky making. Then indeed she was an important young woman.

Anna's *Lebkuchen* and *Anis Plätzchen* were something to dream about quite different from Mrs. Pickrell's alluring ginger cookies, but they were Christmas cakes so outstanding that I have remembered them and their making all my life.

We youngsters thoroughly enjoyed Anna's cooking, for she was most indulgent and merry while she creamed butter and sugar, whipped eggs, or sifted flour, meanwhile relating delightful, entrancing fairy tales that gave her as much joy as it did us. Furthermore, she was never overly thrifty in scraping the mixing bowl, so there was always plenty of the rich batter sticking to its sides for the fortunate one whose turn it was to lick it.

Yes, it was a gala day when Anna made a cake, and almost as jolly when cooky making was in progress. Sometimes she wanted the kitchen all to herself, but occasionally she would allow Emil to come in and help her crack nuts or chop fruit, and as I grew older and began to develop a real flair for cookery, she often invited my assistance, thereby flattering me tremendously.

Once inside the sacred portal, with freshly scrubbed hands and immaculate white apron, I helped cut the cakes, put them in the pans, and if I was very careful, I could slip the hot cookies fresh from the oven on to the big cracked turkey platter to cool. I loved that, for all those which had taken on too deep a shade of brown to please Anna, or others that didn't look quite fine enough to appear on Mother's table, I might eat, or save for a party with Millie Andress when my important work in the kitchen was finished.

The real business of Christmas cooky making in our kitchen however, began several weeks before the great day

itself. It began with the arrival of Anna's mother to super-
intend the inauguration of Christmas, which meant the
mixing of the dough for the *Honigkuchen* that later would
be baked by the dozens for the holiday celebration. It was
one of the most joyous days in the year, for Anna's mother
liked children; she even liked to have them around when
she was mixing cakes, so it was a matter of course that
Kitty and I were to remain in the kitchen during the rite.

Anna, and sometimes Emil, called Mrs. Boogenhaugen *Mutter*, but we youngsters had another name for
her which amused her hugely. We called her "The Round
Lady," a title born in our very early childhood before we
could even attempt her name. It suited her peculiarly, too,
for she was very short and very plump, and because of the
four stiffly starched petticoats, to say nothing of one or
two flannel ones she wore under her four-yard-round
dress skirt, she presented the appearance of a rubber ball;
and "The Round Lady" was much easier to say than "Mrs.
Boogenhaugen," anyway.

So, then, about the beginning of December, Anna's
mother would arrive to begin the cookies, and all through
the day our kitchen would ring with cheerful talk, much
laughter, and poking of fun, both in English and German.
As soon as she had divested herself of several of the most
dressy petticoats, laid them out on a chair in the dining
room where everyone could admire the handsome crocheted lace trimming, and changed her woolen dress for
one of gay calico, she was ready. Anna, meantime, would
bring forth molasses, honey, and flour; and after much discussion in two languages as to quantities, for no one had
ever thought to put the receipts in writing, the molasses
and honey were measured out in equal parts and put on the
stove to boil for five to ten minutes. Mutter stirred the
mixture well during the boiling and when it nearly reached
the top of the saucepan, she would throw in a little cold

water and let it boil up once more. Then she would take the kettle, smelling like all the good molasses candy in the world, from the fire, skim the sirup carefully, and set it out of doors to cool in the snow. We always seemed to have plenty of snow when Anna's mother and Christmas came, in the eighties.

At this point another argument usually took place. Should the spices go in now or later? They never could quite remember. Finally they would decide that as the dough was to be made into many different kinds of cookies, each with a different flavoring, it must be later, so all would be serene again, and Anna would bring the flour, sifting it in slowly and carefully while Mutter stirred until the mixture was so stiff that even her strong arms could stir it no longer.

Then—this was the interesting part—then it was turned out on the immaculate table, and four sturdy fists would knead it, pound it, pummel it, beat it to a puttylike consistency, when it would be put to bed in the largest bowl our pantry afforded, tucked under a clean white cloth and set snugly away to rest and ripen for several weeks.

Anna's mother would breathe a sigh of complete satisfaction as she watched the bowl being borne away. Then she would turn her attention to other things.

A week before Christmas, Mutter would again arrive on the scene, this time to finish the cookies. The great bowl of dough would be brought forth from its snug repose in the milk room and divided into sections. Then seeds of various kinds—anise, cardamon, caraway—with spices, fruits, sliced almonds, and other nuts, would be added as memory dictated and kneaded in thoroughly. After this Anna and her mother would roll the dough a section at a time into thin sheets and cut it in stars, circles, hearts, Christmas trees, holly leaves, and other forms. The last step was to decorate the cakes with slivers of candied peel, raisins, or halved nut meats and bake them. Some of the cakes they would bake plain, to be ornamented later with icing, comfits, grated chocolate, or fruits.

The operation was a long but fascinating one, and at its close every platter, tray, and plate we owned, it seemed would be piled high with the spicy, delicious *Honigkuchen* to stow away for our own holiday enjoyment, or to give to friends on Christmas Day. They kept fresh a long time, these substantial cakes, growing even better as the weeks rolled by.

Late in the afternoon, when the baking was finished and the kitchen, made as clean as a china cup, was redolent of spices and honey and fruit, Anna would put the kettle on and make a pot of coffee, and Emil, scenting its fragrance from the carriage house where he was probably at work on a bit of wood carving as a Christmas gift for Father, would steal in bashfully to be greeted vociferously by Anna's mother, and we would all seat ourselves at the newly scoured table and have the most delightful time in the world eating the not-so-perfect cookies and drinking much coffee, theirs almost black but thick with sugar, ours just as richly sweetened but tempered with much hot milk. Then Emil would hitch Daisy and Dolly to the cutter and take Anna's mother, laden with much booty in the shape of gifts of homemade sausage, jam, apples, and, of course, cookies, to her home on Clybourne Avenue.

At Christmastime, when the yuletide cakes were in the making, Anna's mother, little roly-poly, lusty-voiced woman that she was, our "Round Lady," was as important and as necessary to us children as Kriss Kringle himself.

Sometimes before she left, Anna's mother would make one of her spicy *Apfelkuchen* or *Kaffeekuchen* for "Vater's breakfast." That Father would not think of eating cake for breakfast did not concern her. She had the time, and the apples were plentiful and conveniently near; therefore she made the cake, but we children, with Anna's help, took care that it was not wasted.

Both Apple Cake and Coffeecake were made in much the same way up to a certain point. There their roads separated and the finished products were as unlike as any two cakes could possibly be. Anna's mother melted half a cup of butter, stirred a cup of sugar into it, and broke in three eggs one at a time. Then she beat the butter, sugar, and eggs vigorously, grasping the spoon as firmly as though it were a plough handle, until the mixture was light and foamy, when she whipped in two cups of flour sifted with two teaspoons of baking powder and ½ teaspoon of cinnamon and a dash of salt, adding a little milk now and then until she had used one cupful. So far the cake might be either Apple or Coffee Cake. The difference began when she turned the batter into a shallow greased baking pan and put on the finishing touches. If a Coffeecake was in order, she would sprinkle granulated sugar, cinnamon, and grated almonds over the surface, using her own good judgment as to quantities. *Apfelkuchen*, however called for quartered, thinly sliced, but unpared red apples, arranged neatly in overlapping rows as a topping, the apples being strewn thickly with brown sugar and bits of butter and nutmeg. These cakes were baked in a moderate oven for about three quarters of an hour. They were heavenly, eaten fresh with a glass of milk, or if you were grownup, a cup of tea, to accompany them. "Plenty goot for company, and not too goot for *Kinder*," Anna's mother would say as she cut us generous slices.

Torten she made for us, too, rich German cakes that were really too fine for everyday occasions, but so delicious one never thought of that. If she would only have yielded to our coaxing, we could have eaten *Torten* three times a day. I think her Chocolate *Torte* was the most popular with us, perhaps because we so enjoyed seeing her make it.

First she called for German sweet chocolate, a whole cake of it, probably weighing from four to six ounces, which Anna broke in small pieces. She dropped these in a bowl, set the bowl in hot water, and placed it on the back of the stove. Then she ground a cup of almonds as fine as meal, while her mother beat the yolks of seven eggs and half a cup of sugar together for half an hour. A full hour, she insisted, was the proper length of time, but—well, in this day everyone was in a hurry, so—.

The chocolate, melted to a rich, brown sirup, and the almond meal were both stirred into the egg yolks and sugar, now whipped to a creamy tint and light as thistledown. The grated rind of half a lemon was also added, and finally the stiffly whipped whites of five eggs were folded in delicately. Anna prepared the pans for the *Torte* in a novel way, we thought. First she buttered two layer-cake pans, then sprinkled them with fine dry bread crumbs. The cake batter was arranged on top of the crumbs, and the cakes were baked about half an hour. It was always a definite surprise to see those cakes come forth from the pans so easily and whole. Each time they were made I feared they would in some magic manner be transformed into a sort of candy, or else would not thicken as cakes should, or that some dire mishap would overtake them, but it never did; the cakes were invariably perfect. Sometimes Mrs. Boogenhaugen would make a loaf cake of her strange batter and coat it with a creamy chocolate icing made of finely powdered sugar and chocolate, with hot water enough to make a paste; but usually if the *Torte* were to be eaten the day she made it, and it usually was, she put the layers together with a lemon-flavored, slightly sweetened whipped cream, and topped the luscious thing with the whipped cream put on in mounds. To make it even more entrancing, she would strew blanched sliced almonds over the cream. Sometimes the loaf cake would be ornamented with an intricate pattern of whole blanched almonds, arranged before the chocolate icing was quite dry. Both forms of the cake were sumptuous, and we could never decide which was our favorite.

After the loquacious and colorful Mrs. Boogenhaugen had finished her pleasant invasion of our kitchen and gone on her merry way, Anna began Christmas baking on her own account, for there were still the *Lebkuchen* and the *Braunschweiger* and the *Anis Plätzchen* to be made. These were her specialties, modestly kept in the background during her mother's more important activities. Lottie, a girl not long over from the old country, had taught Anna to make these cakes, but because they were somewhat less complicated and more quickly finished than her own traditional *Honigkuchen*, Anna's mother would have nothing whatever to do with them. They were not made as the old true German *Kuchen* should be made; also she had no faith or confidence in written receipts. If a cake was good, its formula should be remembered, even down to the smallest caraway seed. But we had a very different opinion of Anna's cakes. They were gorgeous, we thought, and our one and only fear was that she might not make them in generous enough quantities.

Anna's *Lebkuchen*, to my way of thinking, is still one of the best of the honey cakes. It calls for a pound of strained honey, 2 cups of light brown sugar, ¼ cup water, ½ teaspoon soda, ½ pound blanched and shredded almonds, 8 cups of flour, or thereabouts, ¼ pound of citron, candied orange, and lemon peels mixed, ¼ teaspoon each of cloves and nutmeg, 1 teaspoon of cinnamon, and 2 eggs.

Anna, assisted by the willing Emil and ourselves, meaning the youngest members of the family, always blanched and shredded the almonds and sliced the candied peels after the supper dishes were washed and put away on the evening before the cakes were to be made. We had a great deal of laughing and yodeling behind the tightly closed doors of the warm, bright kitchen as we worked. It was very cozy there, the lamp chimneys shining crystal-clear, fresh, starched curtains at the windows, the wire plant stand filling the air with the scent of geraniums and heliotrope, our chairs drawn up to the table where all the good things for the cooky making were arrayed almost too temptingly, and nine o'clock came all too soon on such enchanting nights.

After Anna had set us to work on the nuts and fruits, she would put the sugar, water, and honey over the fire to boil for five minutes or so, then she would set the sirup aside to cool, while she turned her attention to the flour sifting, for it took some time to coax eight full cups through our old flat sifter. By the time she had added the soda and spices to the last cupful and stirred it in well the honey would be cool, and she would add the flour, and the eggs one at a time, the nuts, and the peels; and Emil would give the whole mass a wonderful stirring with a stout wooden spoon. Finally Anna would pat it into a loaf, cover it with a cloth, and set it in the milk room for the night.

Then, if we had been diligent and finished our tasks before the fateful bedtime, Anna would make some of the dough into little balls, press a raisin or nut meat in each one, and bake them quickly. *Pflastersteine*, or cobblestones, she called these cakes, and hot from the oven with a mug of sweet cider they were the high point in a happy evening. Even cobblestones in our stomachs had no power to disturb our blissful slumbers.

After we had gone to bed, Anna usually made a batch of *Braunschweiger*, another of Lottie's importations, as the dough was far more simple, and there were no nuts or fruits to prepare. The next evening, when we were again ready to help her, all the cakes would be cut and baked at once.

⤜ BRAUNSCHWEIGER ⤛

2 cups brown sugar	1 teaspoon soda
½ cup honey	1 egg
⅓ cup butter	1 tablespoon lemon juice
4 ½ cups flour	1 tablespoon grated lemon
1 teaspoon cinnamon	rind
¼ teaspoon each mace and	2 tablespoons milk
cloves	

"Mix the honey with the sugar," read the directions in Anna's book. "Heat over the fire but never boil, just melt. Add the butter, lemon juice, and rind then cool. Beat the egg, mix it with the milk, and stir into the honey and sugar. Sift the flour with the spices and soda, throw into your bowl, and stir good. Leave to stand all night. Next day roll out and cut in square cakes, sprinkle over with sugar, and bake fifteen minutes."

And next day we did roll and cut into square, round, or oblong cakes, both the *Braunschweiger* and the *Lebkuchen*, until our arms ached. That is, Anna did the rolling and most of the cutting, but we children had our share in it all, too. When they were baked, Anna let us cover them with the simple icing she made by mixing the finest powdered sugar to a paste with water and a few drops of vanilla or lemon for flavoring. Before they were quite dry we sometimes sprinkled them with crushed barley sugar, or comfits, or chopped nut meats, or bits of green transparent citron, and often we made the initials of our friends on the cakes. These were put away separately to avoid confusion when the Christmas boxes were prepared. Once Anna made a splendid great cooky marked with Emil's name in red sugar and a red sugar border. It was wrapped in paper and hidden very carefully until Christmas morning, and we had to promise to keep it all very secret.

When Anna made *Anis Plätzchen* we had to be very good and quiet, for *Anis Plätzchen* were what she called crotchety. She said she needed all her eyes to make them come just right. The making was so interesting, though, and we were so fascinated by it that it was no hardship at all to be very patient and still. First Anna would set a bowl in a pan of hot water on the stove and break four eggs into it, then she would add a cup of powdered sugar and beat until the mixture was quite warm and so light it would rise nearly to the top of the bowl. When this happened she spooned in two cups of flour, a good pinch of salt, and half a tablespoon of anise seed, and mixed everything together very thoroughly. Meantime I would rub the baking pans with soft butter to have them quite ready for the cakes, which Anna dropped from the end of a spoon in neat little rounds. She didn't bake them then; no indeed, *Anis Plätzchen* must wait in a cool place until a crust had formed over each one, which would take three hours or longer. Then Anna would bake them very carefully in what she called a slow oven, in order to keep them a nice yellow tint. They were very dainty cakes, almost as though made of lace, but, as Anna said, "crochety."

Had it not been for Emil, Springerles would have been entirely absent from our assortment of German Christmas cakes, for Anna lacked the proper tool to make them. "It is such a rolling pin," she explained, "such a big rolling pin with pictures on and marked out in squares so you always get the cakes just right and with pictures on from the rolling pin. Even Mutter has no such a rolling pin yet once."

It sounded rather vague and confusing to us. How the pictures might be transferred from the rolling pin to the cooky dough, we could not understand, and Springerles immediately assumed the most tremendous importance to us. They were like the pot of gold at the end of the rainbow, and seemingly just as elusive. Anna, deaf to all our pleading, simply would not make the cakes other than according to tradition, and unless she could go back to Germany and find "such a rolling pin with pictures on" there seemed no way in the world to gratify our curiosity.

However, when I was about twelve, and Emil had heard the Springerle lament through three Christmas bakings, he one day called me into the little nook in the carriage house where he carried on his own private enterprises, among which wood carving held a prominent place. "Please, you see," he said shyly, and showed me a thick, smooth oak board, marked in squares, with rather crudely carved pictures ornamenting each square—birds, flowers, fish, stars. "You think Anna can use as good as rolling pin?" he asked, and then I knew that at last Anna would have no excuse for omitting Springerles from the cooky collection.

Such rejoicing! And Anna must go that very evening to display Emil's handiwork to her mother, who received it enthusiastically, although I am sure it was not quite according to tradition, for Emil had made it entirely from memory and Anna's confusing description. But that Christmas and every Christmas thereafter as long as I can remember, we had Springerles, for Anna's mother had the receipt in her head, and Anna had the wit to write it in her book. Here it is:

⟳ SPRINGERLES ⟲

2 eggs
1 cup sugar
1½ cups flour

Oil of anise seed, a few drops

Simple enough, to be sure, but entailing an enormous amount of work. Anna first beat the two egg whites until they were just frothy, then added ¾ cup of sugar, and continued beating for half an hour by the clock. Meantime, as I was a big girl and could obey instructions, I was set to work beating the yolks of the eggs with ¼ cup of sugar for the same length of time, privately hoping the Springerles would be good enough to justify my aching arms. Then the two egg mixtures were combined and Anna beat them for half an hour longer. Beating was very important, she told us. Next the anise oil was dropped in very gingerly, and the flour added in small amounts. When it was all in, Anna kneaded the aromatic dough a bit, then rolled it out—and she was ready for Emil's Springerle board. We all stood round wide-eyed and openmouthed to see how it would work, or whether it would at all, for certainly it was not "such a rolling pin."

It was a breath-taking performance for every one of us. Anna dusted the board with flour and pressed it firmly on her sheet of dough. In a moment or two she lifted it— and there, sure enough, were twelve square cakes, each with a little raised picture on its surface, as plain as day. When Anna had cut the cakes apart and baked them in a very slow oven to a pale yellow tint, they were honest German Springerles. Even her mother had to admit that.

We children were a little disappointed, I remember, for the cakes were as hard as rocks, but Anna said with patience and waiting they would become soft. Perhaps they might, but who were we to resist any sort of cake, adamantine though they might be; so we never learned from our own observation whether Anna was right or not.

What waffles mean to the present generation, Anna's breakfast cake meant in the days when I was growing up. Seldom a Sunday morning from early autumn to late spring but this persuasive cake, fresh from Anna's oven, made its appearance on our breakfast table. Tender, delicately spicy, and just sweet enough to add zest to that last cup of coffee, it appealed even to Father, who usually considered sweet cake for breakfast almost indecorous. "But of course," he would say by way of alibi, as he helped himself to the last bit on the plate, "of course this cake is only moderately sweet." So on Sunday mornings we had Anna's cake for our breakfast and I can still recall the tormentingly inviting perfume it sent through the whole house as we youngsters scrambled into our stiff, starched Sunday-school attire and with rustling petticoats hurried ourselves to the dining room before the grownups had devoured it completely. And this is the way Anna made her Breakfast Cake: Two cups of flour, a good pinch of salt, and ¼ teaspoon each of nutmeg and cinnamon were sifted together, then mixed with a cup of sugar. With her fingers she would next rub in ½ cup of shortening, sometimes butter, sometimes lard, sometimes a mixture of both. As soon as the flour and shortening had reached the stage where it looked like small peas, she would take out half a cupful, and to the rest add two teaspoons of baking powder, stir that in well, then moisten the whole with a cup of milk mixed with two well-beaten eggs. Anna would stir all vigorously for a few moments, turn her batter into a well greased shallow pan, spread it smoothly, sprinkle her half cup of flour peas all over the top, add a sprinkle or two of cinnamon, and if she had them, a few chopped nut meats. The cake baked in about thirty-five minutes and was ready to accompany the coffee and eggs to the breakfast table, steaming hot, when Anna rang the breakfast bell.

Christmas!

*A*LTHOUGH when my sisters were old enough to take a real interest in cooking, Mother relegated much of the cakemaking to them, there were certain important, almost ceremonial, cakes that she would trust to no other hands but her own. The Christmas Fruitcake was one of them. I suppose my recollection of this cake and the pleasant bustle and excitement that attended its mixing and baking is the clearer because it heralded a season of such delightful mystery, such unique joy for me, that neither time nor any vicissitude of fortune that has since overtaken me has ever had the power to eradicate the memories of those ecstatic days.

Along about the time of the first snowfall Kitty and I would be seized with the "Christmas Feeling," which we were never able to describe, even to each other. It was a strange sensation that seemed to start way down in the pit of the stomach, leaping and bounding upward through the heart, until finally it bubbled forth in little long-drawn squeaks; and we would assure each other, in the words of a modern newspaper advertisement, "Only so many days before Christmas."

Then, panic-stricken that time was flying so fast, we

would begin our gift making. So much to do, so many friends to remember, we must not lose a minute. Hastily, even feverishly, we got out the scraps of silk and velvet; the bits of ribbon; strands of embroidery floss; sheets of perforated cardboard, white, silver, gilt; gay beads and bright-hued buttons; and all the other treasures we had long been hoarding for this glad occasion, and proceeded to transform them into court-plaster cases, pin-cushions, needle books, tidies, bookmarks, and what not, to present to our relatives and friends on Christmas Day.

It was a most entrancing occupation. Many earnest whispered conferences as to who should have hair receivers and who bookmarks, and whether a pink tidy or a purple pincushion would be most prized by this person or that, were necessary. We longed for Emily's advice, but feared to betray our secrets even to her. Because Mother, Aunt Sophie, our elder sisters, and Anna were all deep in their own private plans, we might snip and cut to our heart's content. No one paid the slightest attention to the litter we left in our wake; indeed, they sometimes even forgot to send us to bed.

Maud, shivering in the cold attic, was at work on a beautiful motto for Mother. "Give Us This Day Our Daily Bread," read the motto, when Maud had it all finished in blue floss with sheaves of yellow wheat decorating the border. Emily was also making a present for Mother, an elaborate fascinator in white wool; so, wrapped in shawls, she kept Maud company in her icy retreat. Mother and Aunt Sophie locked themselves in the sewing room, busy with black alpaca aprons trimmed with many rows of scarlet braid, which we sisters, all five of us, wore with an air on Christmas Day. Anna's secret almost invariably proved to be gay wool stockings for each of us, knit by her own devoted hands.

Molly could never quite decide which group to join in

these frenzied gift-making activities. The attic was chilly, and, besides, she had no hankering to work mottoes, nor to crochet fascinators; on the other hand, Kitty and I were merely little girls, while she was almost, if not quite, grown-up, and therefore she was a little fearful her dignity might suffer if she spent her evenings in our society. Usually she did, however bringing her own garnered treasures with her and astonishing us by her cleverness. What splendid gifts Molly could create from scraps of silk, buttons, and beads!

The entire month of December was filled with mysteries and thrills, and the "Christmas Feeling" grew so intense that it seemed to poor little Kitty and me that we would never be able to contain ourselves until the great day arrived. There were such ravishing goings-on everywhere. Something swathed in sheets loomed big and ghostlike in the attic chamber, and we were warned not to open the door, nor even to go near the room. In the barn Emil would hurriedly get his fat little body in front of a thing that looked blue, and again red, whenever we skipped out to chat with him. And packages from Canada, or the North Pole, for all we could discover, would arrive by express and be spirited away before we could say Jack Robinson. It was all so excitingly lovely.

Every night Kitty and I, very wide-awake, would toss on our bed for hours, speculating, wondering, wishing, until to calm our seething minds and perhaps make Christmas come quicker, we would cuddle down and tell each other stories, a favorite pastime with us. We had one tale that was endless—"Nelly's Doll House," we called it. "Nelly's Doll House" was a joint romance. Either one of us would take it up where sleep had overtaken us the night before and carry right on until the Sandman brought the chapter to a close.

What a wonderful, magnificent house Nelly had! All

the modern improvements we had ever heard of, plus a great many more inspired by our imaginations, were hers. Chairs set with diamonds and pearls; sofas that played sweet music as the dolls seated themselves upon them; carpets on which grew real but diminutive roses, violets, and lilies; golden cradles for the baby dolls; kitchens equipped with stoves that really baked delicious cakes for the doll family; and churns wherein real, actual butter might be made. The doll family rode doll horses which cantered and loped just like Daisy and Dolly. There seemed to us nothing, however fantastic, that we did not contrive to give Nelly for her doll house.

It was a happy time. Uncle George hummed old carols and teased us about Santa Claus, his twinkling eyes bluer than ever. Aunt Sophie beamed on everyone and innocently betrayed our most cherished secrets in her own naive way. We children haunted the kitchen to gaze at the old clock, counting days and hours, but while we pined for Christmas Day to speed its coming, we deplored the fact that after all, when it did arrive, it could only last as long as the clock's calendar would permit.

Father alone was sad, even morose. In fact, he pretended to despise Christmas and all its attendant merriment. From the day we began our joyful preparations he wrapped himself in gloom and retired, to quote Mother, into "one of his humors." Notwithstanding his dejection however, he brought quantities of good things into the house, raisins by the box, drums of figs, French prunes in silver-paper wrappings, combs of honey, brandy, cordials, hams, nuts of every description, a bright-hued Edam cheese, and other luxuries whose names were totally unknown to us. In silence, asking no help and accepting none, he would store everything away in the milk room. Afterwards, with a slightly martyred air, he would take his place at the supper table, sometimes actually refusing (we thought to drive home his grumpiness) a second helping of deep-dish apple pie with clotted cream, his favorite dessert.

Each year Father gave orders that we were to expect no Christmas celebration. That was final, and we were sternly asked to remember that his word was law. But Mother went on with her plans as placidly as though he had not spoken at all. As for the rest of us, we had heard that wolf cry, "No Christmas," so often that it failed to impress us, and since Mother took it all serenely, we continued our gift making (though not in his presence), not forgetting to make Father's annual court-plaster case and bookmark exceptionally handsome.

We never held Father's grouchiness against him. We understood its cause and were very sorry about it, but the fact that our baby brother had died years before we were born could not damp our spirits eternally. Christmas was almost here and we were thankful that Mother's sadness was of a more tolerant nature and not quite so enduring.

So we avoided Father whenever it was possible, at other times showered him with grimly received attentions, and left the rest to Mother, which was very wise, for sure enough, quite early on the afternoon of Christmas Eve he would come home roaring for Mother to put on her bonnet and shawl and go to the city with him, and then we knew that once more Christmas was saved.

Late that evening they would return laden with bundles, and next morning, when long before the stars had disappeared, we went scampering through the house shouting, "Merry Christmas!" there in the front parlor, would stand a tree, blazing with candles, its tip almost reaching the ceiling, decked with all the favorite old ornaments and tinsel gewgaws and a hundred new ones, cornucopias filled with nuts and candy, oranges and red apples and sticks of peppermint candy dangling from its branches.

141

"Such a tree! The finest we have ever had," Aunt Sophie would remark year after year.

And now all the secrets were out. The mysterious ghostlike object in the attic chamber proved to be a doll house, a veritable "Nelly's Doll House," built by Emil and furnished completely by Emily's deft fingers, even to a tiny piano of stiff pasteboard, brown paper-cambric in the parlor, and a churn in the kitchen. A little cupboard, painted blue, with Kitty's name on it, was one of Emil's secrets; the other a sled with my initials in a circle of red birds. Anna's stockings with stripes going round and round were very handsome, though they did emphasize my lusty legs, as Uncle George lost no time in mentioning, in his sportive manner, but I was too happy to be annoyed by his teasing—for wasn't it Christmas?

After we had let the "Christmas Feeling" have its way with us and had emitted so many joyous shrieks over each gift that we were almost breathless, furtively eaten a few pieces of candy (strictly forbidden before breakfast), and donned our gay alpaca aprons, we had to present our tidies and hair receivers and other tokens, and to our great satisfaction they were received with all the enthusiasm and expressions of wonder at their beauty and our cleverness that we had hoped for and confidently expected. Anna and Emil, who shared our Christmas-morning gladness, were made happy with presents from everyone from Father down, and these of course we would have to examine, with more exclamations. It was all so exciting we could scarcely eat our breakfast when Anna, in one of the gleaming new white aprons Mother had made for her, her cheeks rosier than ever, called us to the table.

There were usually one or two stars still twinkling in the sky when Mother would announce to Emily in a startled voice that it was high time to get the plum pudding over the fire; and then, followed by Aunt Sophie, Emily,

Maud, and Molly, she would hurry to the kitchen to prepare the great feast of the year, and Kitty and I would sally forth in the chill early light to deliver our gifts. By the time we had visited the Pickrells, the Warners, and all the rest of our especially dear friends, the sun would be shining on the glistening snow, or perhaps it might even be snowing, which made it jollier. When we reached home and got ourselves unwound from layer after layer of wrappings, we would find that most of the Christmas dinner guests had arrived—Mrs. Alcott, Miss Lizzie Dexter, the Serenus Hales, Cousin Ellen, and perhaps a friend or two of Father's stranded away from home over the holiday. Often our guests equaled our own number, and it was necessary to stretch the dinner table to the very limit of its capacity.

More gift exchanging, more ejaculations, more "Thank you's," until everyone had talked himself out of words. It was a merry, gay time, with Father making jokes and acting as jolly as though no such thing as a humor could ever possibly have had a place in his pleasant, genial ego.

And then came the enormous Christmas dinner, with one, or possibly two, prime turkeys, plumply full of the only kind of stuffing Mother ever gave us—homemade bread, finely crumbled, moistened with plenty of melted butter, seasoned to a nicety, and flavored with sweet marjoram or summer savory. Mother would not insult the delicate meat of a turkey with sage or onions, though she used them both plentifully in the aromatic stuffing that oozed from the fat ducks which, to Father, were always a very necessary side dish, just as he insisted that a noble baked ham must occupy the place of honor opposite the turkeys. Father had very definite culinary ideas. Cranberry sauce that was really sauce and not an inane though refined jelly, was also one of Father's favorite dishes. In fact he declared that cranberries as Mother cooked them were more to his liking than strawberries or peaches, and second only to rhubarb or gooseberry in his estimation.

We had plum jelly in quivering crimson mounds to eat with the ducks, and vegetables were placed in every conceivable spot not taken up by pickled peaches, celery, and other knickknacks, up and down the long table. I usually tried to avoid these in order that I might eat more of the turkey, ducks, and ham, and still keep sufficient space for the plum pudding (made by Grandma McKenzie's own receipt) which would make its appearance at the proper moment, wreathed in flames and decked with holly. We would smother it in sherry-flavored hard sauce, or drench it in brandy sauce, and everyone would try his best to catch a teaspoonful of the blue flame that Mother ladled over our portions, for there was a tradition in our family that whoever could accomplish this feat would have nothing but good luck until the next Christmas.

There was mince pie, too, rich, spicy and containing enough French brandy to please even Uncle George, who vowed that most mince pies were anemic things, not worth wasting one's time upon. Figs and nuts and handsome layer raisins came in with the dessert also, and there was claret or sherry or port for those who wanted it, and now and then, when times were very good, champagne. We feasted merrily on Christmas Day in our household.

After dinner we, or some of us, would go sleighing. Father would invite each in turn, beginning with Aunt Sophie who usually liked to nap a bit after her colossal dinner. Uncle George, who detested cold weather, excused himself on the plea of having a poem to write, but as he had once told Mother privately that he would be quite as comfortable at home jingling a few bells, with his feet in a bucket of ice water, as freezing to death in the cutter, we quite understood. Mother, too, mindful of the Christmas supper, remained at home, but the rest, snuggled under the buffalo robes, rode merrily away.

It was always difficult for me to decide whether sleigh riding with Father or helping Mother with the supper preparations would be the most fun. I loved skimming over the smooth, hard snow to the merry tune of the sleigh bells, but watching the slicing of the Christmas Fruitcake was a fascinating thing, and there were always crumbs of cake and bits of icing that might be picked up by a watchful child who was close by. Usually I decided in favor of the cake, for, I considered, I could go sleigh riding another time, while waiting for Christmas was a long, tedious job.

The great cakes, for there were always two of them, filled with fruits and pungent with spices, had been hidden away in stone crocks with sweet apples tucked beside them, since the Thanksgiving holidays. Mother would have preferred to make them even earlier, but remembering Father's predilection for afternoon bites and before-going-to-bed snacks, she did not dare to leave temptation in his way too long.

Promptly on the morning after Thanksgiving, Mother and Emily would drive to town for such things as were needed to fill the gaps left by the holiday cooking. During their absence Aunt Sophie kept us busy dusting the house and putting it to rights and getting out utensils and pans and other equipment used on this occasion only. I always loved the smell of Mother when she returned from one of these winter excursions—it was a combination of fresh, cold air and old mink coat, that seemed to me like no other good smell in the world. Mother's coat had seen many years of service and was quite bare as to fur about the collar and cuffs and down the front edge, but we children always spoke of it in capital letters. MOTHER'S MINK COAT was a garment to be respected and revered, for it had once cost Father a great deal of money, and besides, it

145

smelled so deliciously. When she came into the kitchen, her arms full of bundles, her face smiling, her cheeks quite red, and bringing in such a wonderful feeling of the outdoors, I used to be very sorry for Millie Andress and all the other children of my acquaintance that they could not have my mother for their own.

Gathered about the long table in the kitchen that afternoon, we five girls, with Mother and Aunt Sophie, would seed raisins, cut them in quarters with the kitchen shears (never were they chopped), wash and dry the currants, crack the nuts, pick the meats meticulously from the shells, dice figs, shave luscious green citron and the other candied peels into wafer-thin slices, sift flour, and do the hundred and one essential things that were to make the Christmas Fruitcakes perfect. Aunt Sophie entertained us with endless reminiscences of her own girlhood or our mother's, which sounded remote and old-fashioned to us, who considered ourselves very up-to-date and modern indeed. Uncle George, who just could not stay away from the kitchen where all this bustle was going on, strolled from one worker to another, teasing us all unmercifully, waggishly pulling long braids and filching whole handfuls of nut meats all measured and set aside for the cake. When we raised an outcry at this knavery, Aunt Sophie would tell him he was a very bad boy and send him out of the room in disgrace. Twilight would overtake us by the time our tasks were finished, and feeling very virtuous, we would carry the good things to the cool milk room until morning, when Mother would begin the actual mixing and baking of the wonderful cakes.

The dark fruitcake was made first, as its baking was a slow process. Three or four hours in the oven, or two hours' steaming, and at least one and a half hour's baking, was Mother's rule. Often, if the oven heat was low enough, she baked it a full two hours after the steaming.

This was her receipt, used every Christmas as long as I can remember:

～ DARK FRUITCAKE ～

2 pounds seeded and quartered raisins	½ cup sherry wine
½ pound figs cut small	4 to 5 cups flour
½ pound finely shaved citron	1 pound butter
½ pound mixed candied orange and lemon peel	1 pound brown sugar
	1 cup molasses
½ pound blanched almonds cut in thin slivers	10 eggs
	1 tablespoon cinnamon
½ pound walnut meats coarsely chopped	2 grated nutmegs
	½ teaspoon allspice
1 pound dried currants	1 scant teaspoon soda
	½ cup orange juice

After the flour had been sifted once, a portion of it was strewn over the mixed fruit and nuts, then the remainder was sifted again with the soda. To the butter and sugar, creamed well, the molasses and beaten egg yolks were added, with 2 cups of the flour. Then Mother beat the mixture hard, gradually folding in the spices. The rest of the flour was added alternately with the liquids, sherry and orange juice, and all beaten as hard as possible. Finally the fruit was turned in and mixed well. Then as a final touch the egg whites, whipped to a standing froth, were folded carefully into the mixture. Mother baked this cake in two large tube pans, which we prepared by rubbing with butter, then lining with paper, which in its turn was brushed with butter and covered with a thin film of flour. When the cake finished baking in a slow oven for about two hours, we peeled the paper from it and drizzled sherry wine or French brandy over it. When it had cooled, the drizzling process was repeated. Mother thought it preserved the cake and prevented the crust from becoming too hard. Then it was wrapped in old table linen and stowed in the crock to await its triumphant appearance on our Christmas supper table.

The other cake was more delicate. It was called a white fruitcake, but we always contended it was golden, not white. It was a more expensive cake, as it called for several rare ingredients, such as candied pineapple and candied cherries, but it was so exquisite, I think we would have made any sacrifice to get them for our beautiful cake. This receipt also made two loaves.

⚛ WHITE FRUITCAKE ⚛

2 cups butter	½ pound candied pineapple
2 cups sugar	½ pound blanched almonds
8 eggs	1 pound Sultana raisins
1 cup sherry wine	½ pound citron
4 tablespoons rose water	4½ to 5 cups flour, twice
½ pound grated coconut	sifted
½ pound candied cherries	

We shredded the fruits and almonds the day before, poured the sherry over them, and left them overnight. The coconut was covered with the rose water and set in a cool place for fifteen minutes. We had to wash all the salt from the butter by squeezing it in cold water, then drying it with a cloth, before it was creamed with the sugar. When it was very fluffy the yolks of the eggs, well-beaten, were added, then the coconut and rose water went in, and the mixture was beaten hard for several minutes, while the flour (no leavening was added) was gradually incorporated. The whites of the eggs, very stiffly whipped, went in next, and at last the fruit and nuts, with the sherry. Mother poured this batter also into two tube pans, set them in a pan of water in the oven, which was only moderately slow, and baked them for two to three hours, or until our broom-straw test told her they were finished. Emily iced the cakes the day before Christmas while Father and Mother were shopping, and they did look wonderfully beautiful, something like snow-capped mountains. When the silver cake basket was filled with delicately thin slices of each, they seemed to add just the crowning touch to our happy day.

We went to our beds on Christmas night worn with joy and filled to the brim with happiness and holiday food. Our responsibility was over, the gift making was finished, and the real delights of the winter had just begun. There was skating on Ten Mile Ditch to be considered; there was a snow man to make; Emil had promised that in some way he would contrive a miniature ice hill in our back yard for coasting; and if the cold continued, he would flood the croquet ground so that we might have the fun of after-supper skating, with Father and Mother joining hands and going round and round in the elegant, sweeping way they alone seemed to be able to do well.

Several times through the winter Emily would have a surprise for us. Now and then it would take the form of a grab bag, when, in some miraculous way, everyone would get the very thing he or she wanted most at the very first grab. Or she might plan a play that we would put on in the attic if the weather was not too cold. Usually she wrote, directed and acted in these plays, and always received much applause from our guests, who included almost everyone we knew, from Captain and Mrs. Hardy and the McAlisters, down to Mary, our washerwoman, and her brood, the quarrelsome Mrs. White, Anna and her family, and Emil.

And naturally there would be all sorts of good hot things to eat when we had trooped down from the chilly attic to the dining room. It was very entertaining.

But I think the winter fun we loved best of all was sleighing, perhaps because Father enjoyed it so heartily.

When the moon was at its brightest he would often marshal us all out to the big sleigh, wrapped up like Eskimos and carrying hot flatirons, for an hour's skim over the smooth, hard-packed snow; or on Saturday afternoons he would take Mother alone, her old mink coat covered with The Shawl, and a thick veil over her face.

The Shawl was one of the dearest and most highly esteemed possessions in our home. It was a beautiful, heavy affair, thick as a blanket, made of pure white wool, embroidered in the corners with large realistic flowers of every shade of the rainbow, and bordered about with deep, knotted fringe, in which the white and the gay-tinted wools blended harmoniously. We had come by The Shawl in a peculiar way. Some years ago Miss Byersford had written Father of a raffle she was inaugurating to collect money to repair the old church—"the church by the way, in which you were married," her letter said. She concluded that she hoped Father would gratify her by taking at least one chance at five dollars.

Of course Father had gratified her, for was she not one of the ladies who Aunt Sophie had said was an old flame of his? And could he refuse to help the church which had given him Mother? But five dollars was a goodly sum in our household; so, generous though he might wish to be, one chance was the best that he could do, and he and Mother looked rather sadly at the envelope containing all that money, when it was addressed and ready to mail to Miss Byersford.

But to the grownups' great astonishment, Father won The Shawl, the great white wool shawl, with embroidered flowers and knotted fringe, which Miss Byersford told him had taken her a year to make. Aunt Sophie always stoutly maintained there had been some shenanigans about the raffle, but we were all very glad indeed to have the splendid shawl, and Miss Byersford was delighted that

150

Father was the winner.

Usually The Shawl, with sandalwood strewn here and there between its thick, rich folds, was carefully sewn into an old pillowcase and kept in a drawer in Mother's bureau, but on exceptional occasions it was taken from its retreat, and Mother or Emily would wear it.

Father, in his great coat, knitted scarf, double mittens, his handsome Dundrearies floating in the nipping air, would help Mother and The Shawl into the cutter and away they would go—bells shining like gold, jingling musically, the horses sleek, spirited, their long flowing tails floating in unison with Father's Dundrearies, enjoying the run in the frost-filled air as petted, cared-for horses always do.

The cutter was Father's pride. It was rather a stylish, gaily painted turnout, with a high curving dashboard, but its capacity was small, so it was seldom we younger children had an opportunity to enjoy its wonders. Mother or Emily were the favored ones, and when it was Emily's turn to accompany Father, she always dressed as modishly and as nicely as she could. Who knows but Father might meet some of his friends in the park, and what wonder if possibly, in the friends' sleigh, there might be a strange, but charming young man to whom Father would simply have to introduce her? Who could tell?

So Emily crocheted a very handsome white hood to correspond with The Shawl, introducing glittering white glass beads into the work, and topping the hood with a sort of coronet arrangement which was most becoming. White wool mittens completed the beautiful white ensemble. The first time Emily wore her sleighing costume, we were very proud of her, for as a last touch she had powdered her face rather thickly with cornstarch, and in our estimation she looked as beautiful as a marble statue, but

VICTORIAN CAKES

Father embarrassed her beyond words—just as the Pickrell boys were passing, too!—by roaring,

"Good Lord, girl, go wash your face! You look like a *breitheamh*," which, we afterwards understood, was his Irish word for ghost.

Christmas Fruitcakes came but once a year, but birthday cakes were an almost everyday affair in such a household as ours, and Mother made the birthday cakes. Everyone was remembered, from Uncle George the oldest member, to Kitty, the baby of the family, not omitting Anna and Emil or the stranger within our gates. Mother made Birthday Cakes for us all. Imposing Birthday Cakes they were, too, with garnitures of flowers or holly leaves as the season offered. Everyone dressed up for a birthday supper, and the honored one was especially honored with a very special bouquet.

Father's birthday bouquet was always incredibly beautiful, we thought. Mother made it on a smooth mound of damp sand on a large glass plate; in the sand she inserted the camellia-like flowers of the lady's-slipper, in alternating rows of pink and white, placing at the apex of the mound a tiny boutonniere of rose geranium leaves encircling sprays of mignonette and a tuberose. After his cake had been cut and the bouquet admired, Father, with a dignified gesture, would pin the little nosegay on his coat.

Those birthday bouquets of Mother's were always delightfully unique, and so, too, were her cakes, which, although they differed for each one of us, were invariably made from the same receipt—a familiar one, just the old-fashioned One, Two, Three, Four cake, which goes this way:

⚮ One, Two, Three, Four Cake ⚮

1 cup butter	2 teaspoons cream of tartar
2 cups sugar	and 1 scant teaspoon
3 cups flour	soda or
4 eggs	3 teaspoons baking powder
1 cup milk	1 teaspoon vanilla or other
	flavoring

Just that simple old receipt, a stand-by in every family, but when Mother made it, her cake resembled a fine pound cake, so carefully did she cream the butter and sugar, so deftly did she fold in the stiffly whipped egg whites, and so delicately did she add the extract, which, by the way, she varied so that each one of us could have his or her own favorite flavor. Raisins were always added to Father's cake, citron to Aunt Sophie's, nuts and spices to Uncle George's, and so on. Emily liked almond, Maud lemon, Molly orange, and Kitty and I declared for chocolate, so Mother omitted a few spoonfuls of flour and added an equal amount of cocoa. Anna and Emil celebrated their birthdays just a week apart, so Mother made a large cake for them and flavored it in true German fashion with anise. After their dinner on the big night, the cake was always carried intact to Anna's home, where it was the center of attraction at their inevitable party.

For a very large, elaborate cake, Mother doubled her receipt and baked the batter in pans of varying sizes. When finished they were all nicely iced and piled in a sort of steeple effect, the smallest at the top. Another coating of icing was then smoothed over the whole pyramid, and before this was quite dry, candies or nut meats were temptingly arranged on it, with a nosegay in the center of the smallest cake. A high glass cake stand wreathed in ivy held the marvelous structure. Sometimes Mother tinted her icing a pale lemon tone with egg yolks, or a delicate pink with beet juice; sometimes, for a real birthday party, she iced each cake differently, which made quite a unique effect.

Oh, there seemed to be no end to the clever things Mother could do when a birthday cake was in order. Indeed, our birthday cakes were only second in importance to the Christmas Fruitcake, and she spared no pains to give individuality to them, and pleasure to us. Perhaps that is one reason why I remember Mother's birthday cakes so well.

Love and Beauty Blighted

I Think I was about thirteen when I had my first encounter with a real affair of the heart. It was a momentous experience. Cousin Eva, who was at that time about eighteen, came to spend the winter with us, and Cousin Eva was in love—terribly, but hopelessly, in love, which added greatly to the interest and romance of the adventure. For some reason, unexplained to us, Eva's parents did not look with favor on her beau, or perhaps they considered her too young to know her own mind—a phrase much in use at that time. Be that as it may, Cousin Eva's love affair was frowned upon in her own home, and she was sent to our big, casual, busy household to be cured of her ailment, and at the same time, although this was an unexpected consequence, to give us the most exciting winter of our young lives.

Eva was plain; no one could possibly deny that. However much we loved and admired her, we were forced to admit that she was not at all what a heroine of a romance should be. Her small, pale blue eyes looked, as Aunt Sophie too candidly remarked, "like burnt holes in a blanket"; her nose, to put it as kindly as we could, was decidedly retroussé, and numerous freckles dotted it and her chubby face. But Eva's hair, if not beautiful, was at least

155

remarkable; it was of that peculiar shade of red that envious people called carroty, but we decided was red gold, and so thick that Eva could twist or turn or wave or curl it after any fashion her fancy might dictate, and there it would remain as though made of wire.

At the time of her visit, Eva was wearing her wonderful hair in fat, loose, upstanding curls which made an aureole of stiff tendrils all around her face. This hair-do was only accomplished by much painful effort. The sturdy stem of a clay pipe was held downward in the chimney of a lighted lamp until it had taken on just the right degree of heat, then Eva would twine her locks about it, holding them tightly in place for just the proper length of time required to produce the sausagelike curls. A risky and tedious job was this heating of the pipe-stem, as I discovered, and one that soon became mine because of my curiosity and sympathy for Eva. I learned by sad experience, too, what holding the stem a moment too long in the lamp chimney would do to those red-gold locks which were Eva's one claim to beauty. On the whole, though, her hair was resplendent, and we were not surprised when Eva told us that a sculptor had begged permission to use her curls on a head of Medusa he was modeling. Uncle George grinned when he heard the story and muttered something about hissing serpents which seemed rather unkind, but it was like Uncle George to make some teasing remark, so we paid little attention to him.

Besides, as Eva said, she had things of serious importance to consider. One of them, and the most serious of all, was the fact that she was in the very depths of poverty, had not a penny to her name, and, furthermore, she was not to receive even her usual small allowance during her entire visit. We all discussed this as we helped her stow away her gloves and ribbons and other finery, turn her dresses inside out, and hang them in the wardrobe. All buzzing like bees, we admiringly placed her handkerchiefs in neat piles, smoothed lace ruffles, and tucked embroidery-trimmed chemises into bureau drawers.

It was while unfolding a red flannel petticoat that we happened across Jim's picture. Eva had wrapped it carefully in tissue paper, tied it with a blue ribbon and then to conceal it from suspicious eyes and also to preserve its elegant frame, had bundled it in the petticoat. Jim was a very nice-looking young chap as I remember, very youthful but sporting a stylish mustache. The mustache, I think, so impressed us that our admiration and esteem for our cousin was increased a hundredfold. After we had all looked our fill at the dashing lad holding his derby hat so jauntily Eva swathed the precious portrait in the petticoat again and hid it beneath a pile of substantial winter underwear.

Then it was that we heard the whole story of her romance. It was quite hopeless she said rather complacently. She had been forced to abandon all thought of running away with Jim, which she confessed she had considered quite seriously. Besides, she had not even been permitted to write him a good-by letter, and she was very much afraid he might do something desperate. And now she hadn't a cent, not even a few pennies to buy postage stamps, so—so—and she burst into tears and hid her face in the red petticoat, to the great detriment of the aureole of curls.

It all sounded tragic, and we sat in deep respect until her grief subsided. Then Emily protested. "Medieval!" she exclaimed, using a word that added much dignity to Eva's plight; and in her usual daring way, our sister straightway decided that it was up to us to do something about it and at once. True lovers like Eva and Jim must not be left to pine and suffer.

But what could we do? Money, it seemed, was the

immediate need, and of money we had but little. However, as Emily said, in one way or another we did manage, each one of us, to acquire a small weekly sum to spend as we pleased, and from that store it was our duty to dedicate a portion to the cause of true love.

Father gave Emily a whole dollar for what he called specialty work, which might mean anything from keeping his always confused and chaotic desk in order, to ironing his best shirt. Maud and Molly picked up varying amounts, from nickels to quarters, for emergency tasks. I had my weekly dime for polishing Father's boots, when he remembered it; and Kitty, by virtue of being the youngest, occasionally garnered in nice little sums by blandishments rather than by honest toil. Altogether we could count on a combined weekly income of at least two or three dollars when times were good, and out of this we gladly guaranteed to keep Eva in writing paper, envelopes, and postage stamps. Furthermore, we promised faithfully to smuggle her letters to the mailbox and staunchly to keep her secret. The question of Jim's letters was a real difficulty until Maud thought of Mattie Church, who, she was sure, would be overjoyed to have a part in our gallant conspiracy. Jim could send his letters to Eva under cover to Mattie, and she would hold them securely and secretly until Eva could safely receive them.

Thus everything was beautifully arranged and all was merry as the marriage bell which Eva counted upon hearing in the not too distant future, and we all patted ourselves on the backs like complacent cupids, and enjoyed ourselves thoroughly.

It was very exciting and delightful, especially when Eva gathered us all, even Kitty and me, into her room to hear Jim's letters—in part, of course. We had never been so near a genuine love affair before, and we found it more fascinating than the most thrilling novel.

Naturally, our plan did entail a good deal of sacrifice, for we had taken no thought as to the number and thickness of Eva's letters, and the postage item did mount up disturbingly. Eva, highly appreciative of our self-denial, was filled with a desire to do something as noble for us, so she suggested a series of beauty treatments, at which she declared she was quite expert.

Beauty treatments sounded strangely entrancing to us. Emily, of course, did on occasion brighten the bloom on her cheeks with the petals from an artificial rose or a bit of crimson tissue paper moistened with cologne, and not infrequently she helped herself to a dusting of powder from the cake of magnesia, Mother's one concession to the cause of beauty, securely hidden from Father's eyes in the little box in her bureau drawer. Maud, too, had been known to add similar touches to her complexion, but beauty treatments, guaranteed to produce soft, lovely hands, shining nails, a skin like Hebe's (whoever she might be), even curly hair and—this attracted me more than any of the other gifts of good fairy Eva, for I was always too fat—a sylphlike figure. It sounded astounding to say the very least.

But Eva promised us all this and more. Indeed, she became so enthusiastic over her plans to beautify her simple little cousins, that she entirely forgot to ask for stamps for a whole week, and Jim's letters accumulated until there was such a pile of them Mattie had to bring them over in her Mother's darning bag.

The attic chamber, which, since Eva's advent, had offered lodgment to Maud and Molly, was selected for the scene of action, and Maud and Molly for the first subjects—perhaps I should have said victims. To encourage them, Eva promised to repair her own beauty at the same time.

We were all excitement as we watched Eva's preparations. With Anna and Emil safely on their way to a Clybourne Avenue party and Mother and Father off on one of their rare excursions to the theater, we had the house, particularly the kitchen, to ourselves, which was fortunate, as Eva's lotions and pastes required as much stirring and cooking as a pudding; indeed, the concoction that ensured lily-white hands did not look at all unlike a pudding as it bubbled away on the surprised old stove.

It was composed of bran, fresh from the bin in the barn loft, a few rose leaves from Aunt Sophie's prized potpourri jar, and boiling water. It was supposed to simmer to a thick faintly rose-scented, poulticelike mass, when it would be set aside to cool, while Eva turned her attention to the second item on the list, the "Dream of Beauty Face Mask."

In all innocence Mother contributed most of the ingredients for the mask. Her secret cake of magnesia, mysteriously obtained by Eva, was pounded and mashed to a powder, then mixed to a thin paste with hot water, perfumed with New Mown Hay, also procured from Mother's scanty assortment of toiletry treasures, poured into a bottle and given into Kitty's keeping with injunctions to shake it well while it cooled.

For those who desired curls (and how Molly, with her Indian-straight locks, did yearn for such adornment!) Eva recommended Quince Cream, which she made by cooking quince seeds, saved from the late autumn jelly making, with sugar and water, to an unbelievably sticky mass.

When this was finished, the lily-white-hand mixture was poured into six little sacks (which I think were salt bags), and we were ready for our initial experiment.

Tiptoeing past Uncle George and Aunt Sophie's room, we crept up to the attic chamber, and Molly, enveloped in towels, was soon being plastered by Eva's skillful hands with Quince Cream. It looked very slimy and unpleasant, but Molly sat quite still and uncomplaining even when the gummy stuff ran down her face and into her eyes. She would have endured anything to achieve curly hair. Then Eva twisted the wet strands into curlicues all round Molly's forehead like so many coiled serpents, bound a strip torn from an old petticoat tightly over the curls, and for extra security wrapped one of her own red ribbons over curls and bandage, and Molly was finished, except for the Dream of Beauty Mask, which all three girls proceeded to daub thickly over their faces. Now they were ready for the last act, that of plunging their hands into the little bags filled with the bran puddings, which we onlookers tied firmly about their wrists.

They were funny-looking objects as they gently let themselves sink back on their pillows, and although we all wanted to discuss Eva's plans for further treatments, and I in particular longed to know when the sylphlike figure that had been promised me might be acquired, it was impossible for the patients to speak, so fragile and given to cracking was the Dream of Beauty Face Mask. So we left them. I took one glance as Emily turned out the lamp and opened the windows, and they did look queer and rather frightening there in the moonlight. I hurried down to my warm bed, where Kitty, tired of all the doings, which seemed silly to her, was already fast asleep.

But those still, white faces and shackled hands did not appear as terrifying to me as they did to Mother a few hours later. With her usual watchfulness over her flock, Mother, on her return from the theater, made the rounds of her sleeping family, even into the attic room, and I have often heard her describe the horrid sight which met her gaze as she opened the door.

"There," she would say shudderingly, "there in the full light of the moon lay those three dead (or so I supposed) girls, all bound and gagged and one of them dripping with blood. Their faces were white as ghosts, and they looked so ghastly and so pitiful, was it any wonder I shrieked?"

And that ended the beauty treatments Eva had so kindly planned for us. It all seemed rather too bad, for we never discovered whether the bran poultices would have produced soft, velvety, lily-white hands, or the Dream of Beauty Face Mask a skin like Hebe's. One result only was manifest and that blatantly so. Molly's curls remained in evidence for weeks, and how queer poor Molly did look with those wiry spirals circling her face! Nothing but a thorough washing with yellow soap and hot water would have been powerful enough to obliterate them and the unpleasant traces of the Quince Cream, but of course we had all been given our autumn shampoos some weeks before, and now Molly must wait until the spring hair-washing ceremony to be rid of those castiron curls.

After the beauty fiasco we decided to remain as nature had made us. Although no one had forbidden us to continue the treatments, the joking and ridicule to which we all, even poor Mother, were subjected, were too much for us. Uncle George, with his twinkles and subtleties and quiet smiles, and Father, with his big roar of laughter whenever he glanced at Molly, and his witty accounts of the whole affair, usually much embellished, were agonizing, especially to my older sisters. Kitty and I soon recovered our poise, but Emily and Maud were in tortures for many a long day, for there was no knowing just what Father would say next, nor to whom he might say it. My one regret at our failure was that now I was never to learn the secret of the sylphlike form Eva had promised me. I worried about that a good deal, but Aunt Sophie bade me forget all about it, for it was nothing more nor less, she was sure, than drinking vinegar, and this she had tried herself when she was young, with no good results whatever, as anyone could see with half an eye.

Way down in the bottom of her dear old heart, how-ever, I think Aunt Sophie sympathized with us, and to take our minds off our humiliation she proposed that Eva should be properly introduced to our friends, at some sort of festivity or other, and Mother heartily agreed. Of course, Aunt Sophie said, our affair would necessarily have to be one of those "hen parties," as she called them, for men were not welcome in our household unless Father him-self invited them, which he seldom did, and almost never were his guests what my sisters would have termed young. But Emily and Maud were quite accustomed to this state of affairs, and Eva, though in a less degree than when she first came into our midst, was being very true to Jim and declared she did not wish to meet other men. So that part was easily and quickly settled and it was decided that our party should take the form of an afternoon tea.

And now the whole family was busy planning, no one busier than Eva. In fact, she proved as expert on the sub-ject of parties as on beauty culture. As her enthusiasm waxed and new ideas began to take hold of her imagina-tion, she almost forgot to write to Jim at all, but this was not as tragic as it might have seemed, for his letters had also grown perceptibly fewer as the weeks passed, so there was nothing at all to worry about.

As usual in our home, a party of any kind meant quan-tities of good things to eat, and the tea was no exception. Emily and Maud discussed salads and cakes with Mother, while Eva busied herself with plans for games and decora-tions. Maud naturally would make her Jelly Kisses and per-haps a Devil's Food. Emily, undecided whether a Watermelon Cake or a Vanity Cake would be more appro-priate for a formal tea, finally made both. Anna had several new varieties of sandwiches to suggest, and Mother prom-ised a pan or two of her famous rusks made very, very tiny, perhaps in fancy shapes.

But it was Eva who furnished a real cake novelty for the great occasion. "Boiled Cake," she called it, and a most divine creation it was, too. Just a bit of airy nothingness, flavored and iced exquisitely as befitted such an ethereal conceit. Eva's Boiled Cake is still a favorite of mine, and of a great many other discriminating cakemakers to whom I have given the receipt, which goes in this way:

∽ Boiled Cake ∾

6 eggs	1 lemon
1 ½ cups granulated sugar	1 cup fine flour
½ cup water	Pinch salt

Eva measured the sugar into a saucepan, added the water, and set the pan on a cool part of the range until the sugar had dissolved. Then the saucepan was pushed forward, and the sirup was boiled briskly to the thread stage with no stirring whatever. Meanwhile Emily beat the whites of the eggs to a stiff, fine foam, whipping in the salt during the process, and when the sirup was boiled just right, Eva poured it slowly and carefully over the egg whites, Emily continuing the beating until the mixture was almost cold. Eva beat the egg yolks to a light, lemon-colored froth, adding the juice and grated rind of the lemon. Then she combined both egg mixtures whipping them together lightly, and delicately folded in the flour which she had sifted several times, and turned the foamy, lemon-tinted batter into a shallow dripping pan. It was baked to a pale tint, then cut in diamonds, iced and decorated. Some Eva sprinkled with coconut. Others were split and put together with the icing, which Eva made in this way:

Two cups of granulated sugar were dissolved in one-half cup of water, a pinch of cream of tartar added, and the sirup boiled, without stirring, to the thread stage. Then it was poured over the stiffly beaten whites of two eggs, a very little grated lemon rind and juice stirred in for a delicate, refreshing flavor, and the whole beaten until almost cold. We thought this icing perfect. It went on the little diamond-shaped cakes as smoothly and evenly as satin, when a smooth, even surface was desired, or in tempting swirls or delicious gobs just as obediently. It all depended, as Eva said, on how long you beat it and how cold it was when you put it on the cakes, and so with one icing, you had plenty of variety.

Eva was so pleased with herself and all the fine things we said about her Boiled Cake that she went right to work on another pet of hers—little cakes that bore the name of Bittersweets. The receipt went like this:

⌒ Bittersweets ⌒

½ cup butter
1 cup sugar
2 squares bitter chocolate
2 eggs

1½ cups flour
1 teaspoon baking powder
½ cup milk
½ teaspoon vanilla

The butter and half the sugar Eva creamed together thoroughly, and with the remainder of the sugar she beat the egg yolks. When both mixtures were light and fine, she combined them with much beating, and added the vanilla. Meantime the chocolate had been melting over hot water, and she stirred it into the butter-sugar-egg combination, then added the milk a little at a time, alternately with the flour, sifted with the baking powder. Last of all she carefully folded in the whites of the eggs, then baked the cake in a sheet. When it was cool she cut it in rounds about an inch in circumference and coated the little cakes all over with icing, some of them with white, others with chocolate icing. Nut meats were pressed into some of the cakes before the icing was firm, which dressed them up and added a pleasing variety.

VICTORIAN CAKES

Both of Eva's cake contributions were highly praised and both became very popular in my sisters' circle, but it was Eva herself, not her cakes, who caused the real sensation among our friends and neighbors.

The tea party started off beautifully. All four girls were gotten up in the latest style—panniered, overskirted or basqued dresses; sequin-trimmed and angel-winged sleeves; high, side-laced shoes of fine kid; striped stockings; and, of course, ruffled and embroidered white petticoats. As a final, dashing touch, Eva donned her most entrancing Ornament, a bangle bracelet made of monogrammed silver dimes given her by her admirers. My sisters, having no admirers, naturally had no bangle bracelets to jingle and clink but they were very genteel in white kid gloves with large pearl clasps.

Eva had suggested that the decorations for the parlors be in honor of Oscar Wilde, a very popular social lion in Chicago about this time; and, of course, they consisted very largely of huge bunches of sunflowers, which the girls had very cleverly made from paper. Sunflowers arranged in our tallest vases were everywhere—on tables, in niches, and here and there on the floor—a brand-new idea and one that gave our rooms a decidedly smart air and impressed our guests enormously. But I think Eva's red-gold hair, which stood out more Medusalike than ever, for we had taken great pains with it that day, impressed them even more.

It all started out very beautifully and decorously, Mother and Aunt Sophie standing with the girls in a ceremonious receiving line which was also Eva's notion and quite new to us. Formal conversation was indulged in for a time, then there was a general exodus to the dining room, where sunflowers, placed wherever a sunflower could possibly find room, shone a welcome.

Of course everyone relaxed a bit over the piles of

savory sandwiches, the salads, the handsome cakes, and the hot chocolate topped with pillows of whipped cream; but still there was a display of manners entirely foreign to our parties, a "prunes and prisms" air, as Aunt Sophie would have said, that gave the event a very fashionable, worldly tone.

No one ever quite knew how it happened that the party, begun so elegantly, suddenly became a hilarious tomboy romp. Perhaps it started when Ida Savage tripped over a vase of sunflowers in the dining room and went sprawling on her face. No one could say afterward, but certain it was that Uncle George, coming in from the offices of the Empire Parlor Bedstead Company in the late afternoon, was shocked to find young ladies chasing each other across flower beds and vegetable patches, and jumping over borders like so many wild Indians, striped stockings tumbling over mud-splashed kid boots, lacy ruffles wallowing in the snow, hair flying, faces scarlet, shouts and laughter, breathless cries of "Tag, I caught you," "You're it," piercing the frosty air, with more shrill laughter. "Loud, unladylike conduct and unbecoming squeals," was Uncle George's description of the revels, later in the evening when we had all settled down and Eva had combed her ruined curls and my sisters had exchanged torn striped stockings and mud-caked shoes for fresh attire.

Father, surprisingly, thought it all a great lark. He had driven into the lane just as a wild game of hide and seek was in progress, caught several girls scrambling up the ladder to the haymow, and had come into the kitchen, roaring with laughter, to ask Mother what it was all about.

We never learned what reception our guests, soiled and disheveled, found waiting for them at home when, finally realizing that even the best party does not last forever, they betook themselves and their bedraggled finery away.

But Cousin Eva found herself a most popular young woman during the rest of the winter, and was so besieged with invitations to parties, to teach the art of pipestem hair waving and the making of her famous boiled cake, that she had almost no time whatever for writing letters to Jim.

"No better cure in the world for calf love," remarked Aunt Sophie sagely, "than plenty of good, wholesome fun."

Royalty in the Spare Room

STRAIGHT FROM OTTAWA, the
capital of Canada, to the shabby old copybook that held
Mother's prized receipts came one which she considered
the gem of her collection. Aunt Emily brought it, with several others, when she came to pay us a visit one eventful
summer. "Princess Louise Cake," it was called, and under
the receipt in Mother's fine, sloping hand, and heavily
underscored, is written, "A rich and expensive cake
—Emily's favorite—very choice."

Today, even to read these words of approbation
brings back to me clearly the picture of our kitchen and the
fragrance of the spices and fruits that went into that very
choice cake, one of the first to be baked in our brand-new
and somewhat terrifying gas stove, which had its part in
the memorable happenings of that strange and exciting
summer.

Hitherto, Aunt Emily had been a sort of Santa Claus
myth to us children, a being somewhat on the order of the
various and sundry princesses of Anna's fairy tales, fascinating, wonderful, but mere whimsies. Of course we had
heard her name many a time, had even been entertained for
hours when laid low with measles or chicken pox, by Aunt

VICTORIAN CAKES

Sophie's stories of this same Aunt Emily's childish exploits and adventures; still, we could not make her seem real. At last, however, we had to believe in her. She was coming all the way to Chicago to visit us, and we entered into the preparations of welcome that immediately began to go forward, with our usual zest and enthusiasm. Company was always a joy to us youngsters.

Never had there been such an upheaval in our home. The whole place must be scrubbed and scoured and polished to within an inch of its life, although the semiannual housecleaning had been finished only a few weeks earlier. But the spring rout had been nothing at all to what went on now. On that occasion Mother was content when everything, having been made spotless and fresh, was returned to its accustomed place. Now, it seemed, we must have all sorts of new furnishings and adornments—stiff Nottingham lace curtains for Aunt Emily's bedroom, and a stylish body Brussels carpet, with roses and lilies spilling all over it, to replace the sturdy old ingrain that had seen service on our spare-room floor for so many years. Maud contributed new covers of white piqué embroidered in chain stitch in rose-colored cotton for Aunt Emily's bureau and washstand. Emily feverishly finished the elaborate pillow shams on which she had been at work for a year, so that they might adorn Aunt Emily's bed. We regarded these shams, portraying Raphael's cherubs, as Emily's masterpiece. They were done in Kensington stitch, the borders being scalloped and heavily buttonholed, all by Emily's clever fingers. As the shams, completed at last, lay on the grass plot to bleach, many of our friends and neighbors stopped to admire and marvel at them. Later, when they were starched until they would almost stand alone, and Anna had ironed them to a glistening whiteness, how beautiful they did look on Aunt Emily's bed, and how well they harmonized with Mother's best marseilles spread!

The parlors and hall were repapered. The ceilings, with their bars and crisscross stripes of gilt paper, looked almost like backgammon boards when they were finished. Then Mother did feel that new china was absolutely necessary, though she hated to mention it, but "Emily was not accustomed to ironstone ware, she was sure, and wouldn't it—or couldn't they—" and so on and on until poor Father succumbed and one evening drove the Democrat wagon to the front door, where he unloaded, among numerous other things, most of them edible, a double set of fine French china decorated with bands of robin's-egg blue and delicate traceries of gold. It was, and still is exquisite, and Mother, overcome with joy and gratitude, gave Father a resounding kiss, which he heartily returned, an unwonted display of affection between our rather shy parents.

"Too expensive—too fine—something cheaper," murmured Mother, and I can see Father's face yet, all grins and what on any other face would be termed blushes, as he replied,

"When we are entertaining royalty, we must do it in royal fashion."

I almost dropped the fragile cup I was taking from its wrappings.

"Royalty!" I exclaimed. "Is Aunt Emily royalty?"

"No, no," Mother answered. "Your father is only teasing because Uncle John, Aunt Emily's husband, is in the Queen's service in Canada, and of course he and Aunt Emily are often entertained at Rideau Hall where the Princess Louise and the Marquess of Lorne, her husband, live. That's all."

All! I fear Mother did not know her children. But you may be sure they, or at least I, made the most of this bit of news. Millie Andress had to hear about our Aunt Emily who was almost royalty, and through Millie the information filtered out to the entire neighborhood. Emil and Anna were driven almost to distraction by our babble of this new aunt of ours and her grandeur, and the portrait of Queen Victoria which hung over Father's desk was studied and consulted so constantly that the rather fattish and mediocre-looking lady in the picture must have been amazed.

To us Victoria was not merely England's queen, she was the patron saint of our home, the autocrat, and in our private opinion, the martinet and despot of our young lives. Father never lost an opportunity to remind us of her exalted rank and greatness, and constantly enjoined us to do nothing whatever that might grieve or disgrace so noble, so eminent a lady. Sometimes it was rather tiresome; especially as the Fourth of July drew near did we chafe under Queen Victoria's rule, for on that day when Millie Andress and our other friends were disporting themselves so merrily with rockets and Roman candles, we might not have a single firecracker or even an innocent torpedo, because they, and what they stood for, were an insult to Her Majesty.

But there seemed to be good reasons, after all, for the tearing up and changing of our home to celebrate the arrival of someone who was so closely associated with actual royalty, and the preparations went on enthusiastically.

The kitchen bore the brunt of the improvements. Its alternations were startling. The nice, durable, greenish-brown walls became a creamy yellow; the old iron sink, with its useful and roomy closet for holding the knife-cleaning board, the huge black pots, and the other necessary but unbeautiful utensils beneath, gave way to open plumbing, something my Mother had yearned for for years; all the shiny copper and pewter dish covers and tinware came down from the wall over Mother's table; the big cupboard was cleaned and restocked; and the contents of the milk room examined and augmented with many unusual delicacies. Finally, as a distinctly modern and sophisticated touch, Father brought home the gas stove, which he and Emil, assisted by several curious and interested neighbors, installed.

Our gas stove was a staggering innovation. Although gas for illuminating had been available in our community for perhaps a year, we had preferred the soft glow of our coal-oil lamps, and I think no one in the neighborhood, least of all Mother, had ever dreamed of replacing the dependable iron coal stove with such a dangerous, fantastic, expensive thing as a gas machine for cooking. But there it stood, that ridiculous-looking gas stove, right in our kitchen and ready to go at the touch of a match. About four feet tall it was, and perhaps two feet square, with four burners on top and a silly little oven below. Mother looked rather dubious when Father turned on a burner and applied a lighted match to it, and Emil and Anna jumped nearly out of their skins when the extinguishing of the light was followed by a loud, explosive pop. Anna gave the thing an evil glance and fell to polishing the lilies on the old iron stove so vigorously she dislodged a bolt; Emil's face, as he fastened it for her, was a puzzle; he seemed an entirely different Emil and one I did not like half so well as the old familiar one.

At last everything was ready, and the day of Aunt Emily's arrival dawned. Mother and Father were to drive with Emil in the carriage, polished to a patent leather gloss, to meet her. This was most impressive to us for the carriage, shrouded in old sheets, spent most of its life in the corner of the barn we grandly called the carriage house, only emerging on important occasions. Emil devoted one day each week to washing, refurbishing, and coddling it, trimming the candlewicks in the lamps, applying a rich, black grease to the axles, and shining the glass in the doors. Our carriage had cost Father all of $400.00, and it was expected to last a lifetime. For ordinary occasions the Democrat wagon or the phaeton were quite good enough.

But Aunt Emily's coming was no ordinary occasion! At seven o'clock on a lovely summer morning, Father and Mother, looking trim and refined, waited on the veranda for Emil and the carriage, while we clustered admiringly about our genteel, good-looking parents.

We waited—five minutes—ten minutes—twenty minutes—but Emil failed to make his appearance, and when Mother went back to the kitchen to give some last-minute instructions about the breakfast, she found Anna in tears, and Emil absent. What could it mean?

Father searched, Uncle George searched, we all searched—but unsuccessfully. Emil was not in the barn nor was he in his room. In fact, he seemed to have vanished, and moreover, to have taken the Democrat wagon and Fanny, Father's dependable old mare, with him. Uncle George reported his carpetbag also gone, so there seemed to be no doubt at all about the matter; Emil had run away! The carriage, still in its winding sheets, stood in its corner of the barn, the horses were neighing for their breakfasts, and Alice, the cow, had not been milked.

No time for speculating or asking questions now. Father departed in the snail-power horsecar, calling to Mother as he left that he would bring Aunt Emily home in a hired hack. Mother took off her finery and milked the cow, Uncle George fed the horses and chickens, and Aunt Sophie, sending the sobbing Anna to her room, began the breakfast preparations. We children busied ourselves here and there, meekly and quietly, as became members of a family overtaken by tragedy.

Such an inauspicious beginning to all the good times we had anticipated! A sketchy breakfast served by distrait hosts to a tired guest who had just endured an uncomfortable ride in a rattletrap hack which had seen many better days!

Could anything have been more disheartening?

But a few hours' rest did Aunt Emily a world of good, and she appeared shortly before teatime, fresh and interested and ready to help solve the mysterious occurrences of the morning. For, of course, we had to tell her the whole unpleasant story of the model hired man who had decamped with our horse and buggy, and of the faithful hired girl, who, never failing us before no matter how great the emergency, was at that very moment weeping her heart out on her bed, a hot flatiron at her feet, cold compresses on her head, and kind old Aunt Sophie administering camphor and smelling salts.

And so, instead of being able to offer Aunt Emily the services of two capable, willing people, whose loyalty and faithfulness were unbounded, we were in the embarrassing predicament of having no servants at all—and that was a pretty kettle of fish. But Aunt Emily just laughed.

"It doesn't take a clever lawyer like you, Robert, to diagnose Anna's trouble," she said. "Anna is in love with Emil! That doesn't give us an inkling as to why he ran off with the horse and buggy, but if he is in love with her he'll soon be back, mark my words. As to the cooking, just give me an apron and let me show you what I can do. I've been yearning for just such an opportunity as this for a long, long time. Send Anna home to her mother to be comforted for a few days at least, and Caroline, let's you and I have a genuine old-fashioned good time in that kitchen of yours."

And then began such an orgy of trying new receipts, of resurrecting old ones, of sampling and tasting and stirring good things over the fire or baking them in the oven, of timid experiments with the new gas stove, which, by the way intrigued Aunt Emily immensely, that we quite forgot she had hobnobbed with royalty, was in fact almost a bosom friend of one of Queen Victoria's very own daughters.

That evening, in place of the elaborate dinner which had been planned to celebrate Aunt Emily's first evening with us, we had tea in the garden, a meat tea, I remember she called it. The white tablecloth was spread on the grass and we all sat round it and passed each other plates of wafer-thin bread and butter bowls of creamy cottage cheese, platters of delicate slices of ham in rich milk gravy, and saucers of currants from Father's pet bushes, mixed with red, ripe raspberries, and of course one of Emily's famous white cakes flavored faintly with rose water. Aunt Emily thought this delightful and promised to teach sister a brand-new Rose Geranium Layer Cake just then the rage at Rideau Hall.

If it had not been for occasional pangs of remorse that we could enjoy ourselves while Anna was so downhearted and Emil probably gone out of our lives forever, I think we children would have voted this one of the jolliest evenings of our lives, and we went to bed jubilant that in spite of her royal associations, our Aunt Emily was not in the least like Queen Victoria of the portrait, nor, indeed, like anyone else in the world.

That merry evening was but the harbinger of glorious days to come, days when Mother seemed entirely to forget her responsible station in life as the head of a large family, and once again become just the gay sister of our very gay Aunt Emily. At first we could scarcely believe our eyes when we saw the elegant aunt for whom we had put our home in its very best bib and tucker, tie a voluminous gingham apron around her waist and proceed to make a marvelously tasty stew for which she alone possessed the receipt, or go poking about among the bottles and jars in the old cupboard, sniffing here, tasting there, whipping eggs, skimming pans of milk, or even washing pots and pans at the new open plumbing sink. It was like one of Anna's fairy tales.

Only now and then did she seem to remember what we expected of her, and clutching the wide skirt of her gingham apron as though it were a train, she would make a deep curtsy to Queen Victoria's portrait, exactly, Aunt Sophie said, "like the ladies who were presented at Princess Louise's or even Queen Victoria's court." Then only did we remember that we had once likened her to that doughty old lady, the Queen.

It was pleasant having Aunt Emily with us, for, aside from her good humor, she and Mother were constantly carrying on the most heart-warming conversations about their young days. It was constantly, "Do you remember?" or "Can you ever forget?" or "Whatever became of that lovely Mrs. Jones-Caldwell?" or "It was the prettiest dress at the ball," or "That hat of Mrs. Crosby's, I thought I should die," and often, oh, very often, the conversation would turn to cakes and tarts and other good things to eat—"That sun-dried apple cake of Maa's" (like most Canadians of that period they pronounced "Ma" like the bleat of a little nanny goat), or "That citron poundcake we used to have at Mrs. Kendall-Webster's high teas——" "these crumpets of Aunt Sarah's"——and then almost invariably we would all flock to the kitchen and in an incredibly short time would be beating eggs, sifting flour, or poking the fire in the old stove, although Aunt Emily, after one or two slightly disastrous mishaps—in one of which the oven door was blown across the kitchen—preferred the new gas stove.

The receipt for Wine Doughnuts was unearthed in an old book of Aunt Sophie's that had once belonged to our great-grandmother. It was rather extravagant, the grownups decided, like so many of the old respected receipts, but far too good to be sunk in oblivion, so they revived it. "Your grandmother," said Aunt Sophie speaking to them as to mere children, "always considered Wine Cruellers a fitting refreshment for any gathering and she made them very often."

"Break six eggs in a basin," so went the old receipt, "and beat to a high froth. Throw in one cup of light brown sugar and beat with the eggs to resemble a batter. As you beat, toss in a good pinch of salt and two large pinches of cinnamon. Then you may add your wine, Canary, Sherry, Madeira, or homemade as you prefer, but let it be a sweet wine and take but one cupful for your use. Stir the contents of the basin well, and throw in your flour by the great spoonfuls to make somewhat stiff. Put flour on your board or table, and toss your dough on it. Roll it out to a thin sheet. Cut in diamonds or squares and mark in bars. Fry in hot fat. When done to your liking skim from the fat and sift over fine sugar."

The Wine Crullers were so popular that Aunt Emily decided to try another slightly similar cake, not quite so fragile, not quite so rich, and more modern. True-lover's Knots, she called these cakes, and this is the way the receipt for their making was set down in her book:

⌘ TRUE-LOVER'S KNOTS ⌘

2 eggs	1½ cups flour
⅓ cup sugar	1 teaspoon baking powder
1 tablespoon sweet cream	A good pinch each of salt
1 tablespoon butter	and nutmeg

The eggs and sugar were beaten together, the cream and softened butter added, then the flour, sifted with the baking powder, salt and nutmeg, was folded in and stirred just enough to make a dough that could be handled. Flour was also sprinkled on the molding board, and the dough rolled out in a thin sheet, then cut in strips about three quarters of an inch wide. The interesting part began when Aunt Emily formed these strips into bowknots and lifted them very carefully into the hot fat.

"Only a few at a time," she warned, "otherwise the bows might be disturbed." They looked delicious as they were lifted from the kettle, each one a tempting nut brown, but they looked even better when Emily had coated them with a simple icing made of fine sugar mixed to a paste with warm water and faintly flavored with extract of lemon or vanilla. Some of the bows she made pink, others white, and some she sprinkled with finely shaved citron.

They were so pretty, so novel and their name so intriguing, we should have enjoyed them if they had tasted only one half as good.

And all these cakes were made to the tune of "She Married a Foreigner," or "I Thought My Heart Was Broken," or "That Was the Time You Were Put on Bread and Water," or "He Never Married at All." It was simply fascinating, but weird as well.

When Aunt Emily made the Rose Geranium Layer Cake, favored of the Marquess of Lorne and first served on the tea table of Her Highness the Princess Louise, there were no reminiscences, for this was a serious cake, and required all one's attention.

ROSE GERANIUM LAYER CAKE

1 cup butter	3 teaspoons baking powder
3 cups granulated sugar	6 egg whites
1 cup milk	Almond extract, a few drops
3 cups fine flour	Rose geranium leaves

The butter, Aunt Emily explained, must be washed in

cold water until every bit of salt was thoroughly removed, then fairly smothered in freshly gathered and well-rinsed rose geranium leaves, wrapped in a damp cloth, and set away in a cold place over night. When the cake is ready to be mixed, the wrappings are removed and the butter creamed delicately, the sugar added gradually, and the mixture whipped to a fluffy whiteness. The flour should be sifted two or three times and the baking powder added to the last sifting. Then the flour is folded gently into the butter and sugar, alternating it with the milk, and dropping in just a whiff of almond extract. Finally the stiffly beaten egg whites are whipped in taking care not to stir too much.

"Meantime," directed Aunt Emily, "prepare your pans, three if you like thick layers, four if you wish them thinner. Brush the pans with softened butter, dust with flour, and lay two or three rose geranium leaves on each. Spoon in the batter evenly, and bake the cakes in a moderate oven, not permitting them to become too brown. Remove from the pans and peel off the geranium leaves."

The filling for the cakes went this way: Boil together 1 cup of granulated sugar and ½ cup of water until the sirup will float in a fine thread from the end of a fork, then pour it over the stiffly beaten whites of three eggs, and continue beating until thick and almost cold. Flavor slightly with almond, and pile between the cakes.

It seemed almost too much to add an icing to this already ravishing cake, but an icing it must have, to be genuine, so Aunt Emily made it after this receipt:

Cream two tablespoons of geranium-flavored butter with a cup of fine icing sugar, adding occasionally a few drops of sweet cream. Whip to a very light consistency, and flavor with two drops of almond.

I shall never forget that first Rose Geranium Layer Cake of Aunt Emily's. It was exquisite, with the icing put on in swirls, rather than smoothly and evenly after the accustomed fashion, and how heavenly fragrant it did taste!

Mother asked the McAlisters over for tea that afternoon, and of course they immediately demanded the receipt for Rose Geranium Layer Cake, so that started it on its rounds of all the good cake-makers in Chicago. Kate McAlister was simply transported by its delicacy, and would have much liked to be the only one in her set to serve it, but it seemed that was impossible, for wherever two or three women were gathered together at their macramé lace or Kensington embroidery, Rose Geranium Layer Cake was the inevitable refreshment, as long as rose geranium leaves were to be had.

But the best cake in Aunt Emily's repertoire, the Princess Louise Cake, she did not make for us until after Anna and Emil had returned and all was explained and forgiven.

Anna came home first, escorted by her mother, our Round Lady, and as always when she was present there was the usual broken English, inarticulate spluttering, with Anna, very downcast as to looks, silently gazing around the familiar kitchen—at Aunt Emily, in one of Anna's own aprons, washing mixing bowls and cake pans at the sink, at the shabby old iron stove, and at the impudent little gas stove. Not at all like our red-cheeked, buxom Anna did she appear, as she stood there so humbly while her mother tried in her own obscure way to clear up the mystery of Emil's disappearance and Anna's grief.

And here was the story as Mother finally disentangled it. Emil had run away, so Mrs. Boogenhaugen stated, because he was very much afraid—afraid of the grand lady, the Tante, afraid to drive the splendid carriage, but most of all much, much afraid of the gas stove, which according to Clybourne Avenue views was not a stove at all, but some species of infernal machine. So he had run away, but he did not tell Anna his intentions.

"*Nein, nein,* he not tell mine Anna, and mine Anna she cry because she not know and she is so *traurig,* so sad but mine Anna she not know why he take buggy and Fanny, and so she tink she never see him again." And with that, tears rolled down the faces of both Anna and her mother in torrents.

But Anna must come back to work, she could not help by crying, and Emil could not be brought back by sadness, and so would my mother please be so kind and 'scuse Anna and make her forget Emil who was so bad boy, and so on and on, tearfully, until Mother suggested coffee and some of Aunt Emily's True-lover's Knots to bring a little cheer into the dark horizon.

More exclamations and guttural appreciation when the Boogenhaugens, mother and daughter, learned who had made the cakes. Our kitchen took on quite a genial aspect as the hot, strong coffee sent its stimulating aroma through the room. Anna insisted on reclaiming the apron Aunt Emily was wearing, and she established herself at the sink, while Aunt Emily proceeded to help herself to a cup of coffee and was soon gossiping away with the Round Lady as chummily as though she were chatting with the Princess Louise herself. So Anna came back to us, washing pots and pans at the sink as usual, licking mixing bowls, telling fairy tales, and to all intents and purposes filling her old niche in our household.

Aunt Emily still insisted that Anna was in love with Emil, but Father and Mother pooh-poohed the idea, and Uncle George and Aunt Sophie declared it was all nonsense. Anna was too level-headed to set her affections on a queer funny little man like Emil, and we children could not imagine anything like a romance existing in our kitchen, right under our very noses as it were, while we remained in ignorance of it.

We all had to change our views the evening Emil returned, however, for Anna transfixed with relief and happiness, seized the poor, bashful little man in her arms and seemed about to smother him with bearlike hugs. Of course her exclamations of joy brought us all to the kitchen, Father as stern as a judge about to condemn a murderer, but the rest of us almost as delighted as Anna herself. Emil was ashy pale and panic-stricken, but still adoring as Father began his avalanche of oratory. Pathetic little Emil, though probably not understanding a word of the tirade, assented meekly. "*Ja, ja,*" he knew he was cowardly, dishonorable, white-livered, everything, anything the Boss might wish to call him. "*Ja, ja,*" he knew he could be arrested, he knew he could be sent to prison, he knew he had shamed us, hurt us, but please look—he had brought Fanny and the Democrat wagon back and he had had much trouble. He was afraid, so he had run away, and he had taken Fanny because Fanny would always come home even without driver, so he would go as far as one day would take him and then he would let Fanny and wagon go back home. But because he start very, very early in the morning, he was very tired, and go to sleep in field in afternoon, and he think how bad he is, so he think he come back home to Boss and to Anna (with a sheepish glance her way), but when he wake up some men are running away with wagon and Fanny, and so he must run too, but they go too fast, and he cannot come home without Fanny and wagon and so he has no money and no carpetbag, and he cannot find German policeman, so he must find Fanny by himself and so he walk long time, perhaps two, three days, and then he see Fanny and wagon by roadside, and men were sleeping under tree so he get in wagon and drive as fast as Fanny can go, but home is long way, so it takes long, long time. *Nein*, he cannot find carpetbag and money, but (with starry eyes) he find Fanny and wagon

and now he find home and Boss and Anna, and——
and——. By that time Mother and Aunt Emily were
almost in tears, but practical Anna, with eyes also like
stars, had been busy setting out cold meat, bread fruit, and
milk for Emil. And Father, after a handshake with his
funny little hired man, shooed us all out of the kitchen,
while he and Uncle George went to the barn to soothe
Fanny's poor tired hoofs with flaxseed poultices.

In the back parlor Mother, Aunt Emily, and Aunt
Sophie discussed the love story, and, after the fashion of
romantic women, began making wedding plans. Aunt
Sophie decided to give Anna her prized china plates decorated with folded china napkins and bunches of cherries,
about the only treasure poor old Aunt Sophie possessed.

So Aunt Emily was right after all, Anna was in love
with Emil, funny, quaint little Emil, and Emil was in love
with her, and the cake, the wonderful Princess Louise
Cake that hitherto had been served only to high officials,
titled ladies and gentlemen, at stately Rideau Hall parties,
found itself gracing a wedding feast on Clybourne Avenue, and moreover, it was made by the grand lady whose
coming to Chicago had so nearly wrecked the romance of
Anna and Emil.

Here is Aunt Emily's receipt for the cake which may
have begun its career as "Princess Louise Cake," but which
ever after was known in our household as "Anna's Wedding Cake."

It was a rich cake, and Aunt Emily baked it in three
milk pans of graduated sizes, using the terrifying gas stove
oven for one of the cakes, and baking the other two in the
old iron stove. These are the ingredients:

PRINCESS LOUISE CAKE

¾ pound butter
2 cups sugar
4 cups flour
12 eggs
2 teaspoons baking powder
¾ pound citron
½ teaspoon nutmeg

¾ pound seeded white
   raisins
1 teaspoon extract of lemon
1 whole grated coconut
¾ pound blanched almonds
   cut fine

We all helped make the cake. Some of us creamed butter, others sifted flour, grated coconut, blanched almonds and cut them fine, seeded Sultana raisins, sliced citron wafer-thin, beat eggs, buttered pans, and watched the ovens—oh, there was plenty of work for everyone, even Anna, who, all smiles and blushes, stood at her accustomed post washing dishes, and Emil, so happy he simply could not stay away from the kitchen, but kept continually running in with coal or wood or some foolish thing no one needed in the least.

Aunt Emily made the cake several days before the wedding, mixing the ingredients in the usual way, adding the stiffly beaten whites of the eggs last, and watching the baking very carefully. The day of the wedding she covered all three cakes with a thick, soft icing and piled them in an imposing tier. Then she sprinkled little silver candies over the glistening white icing, and finally brought out her surprise, two little cloth-bodied dolls with shining china heads, one dressed in full bridal array, the other in accepted Canadian fashion for bride-grooms and placed them in the center of the topmost cake, spreading the bride's long veil gracefully over the side.

And how happy Anna was when Emily, driving the Democrat wagon with the rest of us youngsters, each clutching our gifts firmly in our arms, piled in the back, carried the wonderful cake to Anna's Clybourne Avenue home, where excited preparations were in progress!

It was a marvelous occasion for every one of us. We had found romance at last!

My Career Begins

As A Family we adored picnicking, real picnicking, the kind that meant much preparation—huge baskets of substantial provisions, bottles of Mother's raspberry vinegar or blackberry cordial; jars of sliced tomatoes dressed simply with salt, pepper, vinegar, and a dash of sugar, and kept on ice until the last moment; one or more of our family specialties in meat loaves—lemon-flavored veal, spicy beef, or delicate chicken; pans of feathery rolls, split and buttered piping hot, then lightly wrapped to preserve their freshness; sometimes a juicy deep-dish gooseberry pie with a pot of clotted cream to accompany it; or sometimes the dependable old freezer bursting with ripe peach or strawberry ice cream; and of course, since we reveled in their making and eating, cakes. All these good things, plus the tea caddy and the kettle, most important to the grownups, were mere necessities when we started out on one of our never-to-be-forgotten picnics.

Boiling the kettle on a fire in the Woods or on the lake shore was an essential part of the ritual of our outings, a task usually undertaken by Father, who, though never by any conceivable whirligig of chance taking part in the preparation of the tea at home, liked to consider himself something of a connoisseur of the brew, and a past master in the art of its making. How carefully he selected the sticks and bits of wood for his fire, how meticulously he heated the teapot, measured the tea and the water, always on the first boil, and how, watch in hand, he timed the infusion, and then how expectantly he waited while everyone sipped critically. When Uncle George and Aunt Sophie, both inveterate tea drinkers, pronounced it perfect, the day was made for Father.

Yes, picnics were real affairs with us. No silly little boxes of sandwiches and insignificant cookies with weak lemonade to wash the dry stuff down—we believed in eating well and often, no matter how much preliminary work it might mean. In fact, I have often thought our enjoyment began the day before the great event, when we all forgathered in the kitchen to begin our planning and cooking. And when the big, well-stocked baskets, covered with clean old tableclothes, the bottles embedded in ice, and all the other necessary paraphernalia waited on the veranda to be stowed away in our conveyances, it was not surprising that passing neighbors should frequently remark, "Looks as though you intended to feed an army."

Naturally, while Aunt Emily was with us we must have a picnic, and she entered into the spirit of the occasion with all her wonted energy, suggesting, overseeing turning her clever hands to any and everything which might contribute to the general fun and good cheer. Where to go was one of the questions that always called for much discussion when picnic plans were afoot, but after carefully weighing the attractions of the North, South and West sides, we unanimously agreed on Evanston, then but a village whose chief, perhaps only, importance lay in the fact that it was the site of Northwestern University. In one of our previous picnics there, we had discovered a charming, secluded little grove on a bluff overlooking the blue waters of Lake Michigan, with a beach of hard, white sand below, ideal for hoop rolling and croquet. It was our favorite spot in all the country round Chicago.

Driving from Lake View to Evanston was no inconsiderable venture, especially with our cargo of human beings and provisions, and we must have made an imposing cavalcade as we set off. Leading the procession was the Democrat wagon, with Father driving, Aunt Emily in the seat of honor beside him, Mother, Aunt Sophie, and Kitty, or another guest, on the back seat, with baskets, ice-cream freezer, and what not tucked away in whatever space could be found for them. The phaeton would follow, Emily as charioteer, Uncle George and perhaps Miss Lizzie Dexter her passengers, more baskets and packages pigeonholed here and there, and one or both of us younger children, hoops and sticks or even more cumbersome toys clutched in our arms, on our hassocks on the floor. Maud and Molly, riding Dolly and Daisy, would bring up the rear.

Usually we made several false starts, for at the last moment we invariably had to turn back for something of tremendous importance that had been overlooked, but that only added to the merriment of the expedition. At last, everything we could possibly need or want having been crammed and crowded into the vehicles we got off, Anna and Emil waving good-by to us from the veranda.

The journey, for journey it was in the eighties, was often enlivened by exciting happenings along the way. It was on the old Green Bay Road which, so it was claimed, led from Lake View to Green Bay, Wisconsin, that we had our first encounter with a bicycle. How we did laugh and stare at the strange object with the strange-looking creature humped over its high, wabbly wheel. The cavalcade had halted while Father dismounted to kill a huge fly on Fanny's neck as the fantastic thing appeared, and its rider steadied himself against the Democrat wagon to ask a question about the road. I remember how embarrassed my sisters were when Father, having given the information, asked naively, "Do the gadflies bother you, too, young man?" But Father, when he played truant from his office for a whole day in the country, was out for a good time, and he intended to have it too, so he broadcast his jokes as the humor seized him, let them fall where or on whom they would.

If luck was with us we would arrive at our grove in the late morning, passing the university campus on the way. Father, with Uncle George's help, would unharness the horses, and then, with Kitty and me gathering sticks and dry leaves, would begin his tea-making operations. Uncle George would wander off in search of poetic inspiration, Miss Dexter, who was usually with us, would set up her easel and get out the proper colors to paint Lake Michigan; and Mother, Aunt Sophie, and any guests who displayed a willingness to do so would start the intriguing business of laying the cloth and setting forth the feast of good things we had brought with us. Of course, there would be much talk of cooking and much exchanging of receipts. On this one occasion I remember so well, Aunt Emily, by dint of digging among Aunt Sophie's old yellowed papers and worn diaries, had found directions in spidery handwriting for Grandmother McKenzie's "Sundried Apple Cake," and immediately decided it would be just the thing for a picnic, as it would carry well and be so nice and substantial. Fortunately, Mother had sun-dried apples in the milk room (she always managed a few of them each autumn, for old association's sake, she said, but really we thought, because Uncle George so loved his dried apple pies), so there was no reason in the world for not making Great-grandmother's cake for our picnic.

The receipt, after Aunt Emily had studied it out, went something like this:

Sun-Dried Apple Cake

Three cups of sun-dried apples were to be washed thoroughly, then soaked overnight in cold water. In the morning they were drained, chopped fine, put over the fire in two cups of molasses, and simmered slowly until thick, when they were set away in a cool place. While the apples were cooling, a cupful of butter, warmed over the steam of the teakettle, was creamed with a cupful of brown sugar, and a teaspoon each of ground cinnamon, cloves, and nutmeg stirred in well. Four cups of flour and one teaspoon of soda were sifted together twice, and three eggs beaten to a light froth and added to the butter and sugar; then all the ingredients were stirred in with a cup and a half of sour milk and the whole beaten well. The old directions called for a large round pan for baking this cake, but Aunt Emily decided that smaller, shallow cakes would be more convenient for a picnic, so she used our regular biscuit pans. The cakes were so rich and moist and good they seemed almost perfect without icing, but Aunt Emily suggested that if we made them for dressier occasions it might make them more tasty to cover them with a white frosting and sprinkle them with chopped nut meats, and perhaps even to add a cupful of raisins and a few of the nut meats to the cake itself.

Aunt Sophie did not agree with her. "The cake is as it should be without all that dressing up," she remarked. "Your grandmother would never have approved of it. But that's the way with you young people, always wanting to improve and spoil things that were plenty good enough for your forebears."

It sounded very queer to hear Aunt Emily scolded and called a young person, but she just laughed at Aunt Sophie, and said she was a dear old dummy, which of course Aunt Sophie did not hear, so that was all right.

But Great-grandmother McKenzie's cake was good

191

iced or not, dark and spicy and not very rich, so one could eat a good chunk of it. We did not quite finish it at dinner, but the rest tasted especially nice with the tea Father made, just before we left, to send us home rested and refreshed.

We had bananas also with our afternoon snack, an unusual and costly delicacy that Uncle George had smuggled in to surprise us. It was rather pitiful, too, Mother thought, for poor old Uncle George had so little money. But that didn't prevent our enjoying every mouthful of them, they were so strange and foreign, the first bananas I had ever tasted or even seen.

The homeward drive in the twilight was a jolly one. Mother and Aunt Emily sang "Buffalo Girls, Are You Coming Out Tonight," Aunt Sophie joining them in her sweet, quavering old voice. We children had never seen our family so merry and gay.

That summer, as I look back on it, seems to have been an unusually festive one. There were tea parties in the afternoon, when the ladies would arrive with their embroidery or their lacemaking at three o'clock, and chat over their work for a tranquil hour or two before Emily and Maud appeared with the silver tea service and plates of hot buttered scones, and the splendid cake basket laden with a variety of dainty cakes, and everyone would exclaim, just as they do today, that their figures would be ruined, but the cakes would all be eaten, nevertheless, or tucked away in chatelaine bags to be taken home to some cake lover there, which was quite in accordance with Victorian good manners.

Aunt Emily introduced some exquisite little cakes for Mother's parties, from a French receipt she had discovered in Quebec where, she told us, more than half the population was French. "Madeleine Cakes" she called these jewel-like tidbits, and she made them like this:

⟨⟋⟍⟩ MADELEINE CAKES ⟨⟋⟍⟩

Four eggs were broken into a bowl, one cup of sugar added, and the eggs and sugar beaten together until just blended, no more. Then the bowl was placed in a pan of hot water on the back of the range where the contents would get hot but not actually boil. During this period the eggs and sugar were vigorously beaten until they expanded into fully three times their original bulk and became quite warm. Aunt Emily would then lift the bowl from the hot water and fold in by tablespoonfuls one and a half cups of twice-sifted flour and one-half cup of melted butter. For flavoring she dropped in a little extract of lemon and extract of vanilla, which gave a sort of mysterious quality to the cakes, she thought. The batter was then poured into a shallow buttered and paper-lined pan and baked in a very moderate oven.

But the best part of the Madeleine Cake was to happen when it was quite cold. Then Aunt Emily cut it in diamonds, fingers, and triangles which she coated with chocolate, coffee, or vanilla flavored icing, or with a brand-new icing that was very original and tasty, and very easy too. It was made by whipping half a cup of plum jelly into the stiffly beaten white of one egg, then adding fine icing sugar with more beating, until it was stiff enough to spread. It had a pretty, pinkish tint and a pleasingly novel tang. Some of her little cakes Aunt Emily split and put together with jelly before icing them, and they seemed to be the most popular of all. "*Petits gâteaux,*" Aunt Emily called her cakes, and they looked adorable, almost like real jewels.

In the evenings that summer there would be people dropping in to call, and everyone sat in the garden or on the veranda, chatting drinking raspberry cup or lemonade, and eating sandwiches or cakes. We children hung about the fringes of the shrubbery where we would escape being seen and sent to bed, but listening and enjoying everything with all our might; sure, too, that if Aunt Sophie or Emily were there we would always come in for our share of the refreshments.

Those evenings, how pleasant they were, with the faint fragrance from the flower garden filling the air, the tempting sips and bites that came our way, and from the house the tinkle of the piano as Maud, sent in to entertain the guests, played "Silvery Waves" or "Convent Bells," or Von Weber's "Last Waltz."

It did not seem as though anything could possibly happen to disturb our tranquillity. Even Father relaxed his watchfulness over his daughters to the extent of permitting my older sisters to ride alone in the summer twilight, though that pleasant pastime ended abruptly, when a young man on a nice white horse cantered up the lane with them one night.

"Only Mr. Gavin, Father," pleaded Maud, fearing a storm, "just the algebra teacher." But although the storm did not descend at that moment, my poor sisters rode no more in the evenings without Father's escort.

But picnics, teas, friendly little evening gatherings, delightful as they were, did not, in my parent's estimation, seem quite adequate to do honor to a lady as aristocratic and accustomed to elegant entertainments as Aunt Emily. Therefore, as the summer waned and her visit drew to a close, they decided to have one really fashionable party, and to give the occasion even more distinction they would at the same time commemorate their twenty-fifth anniversary, their silver wedding.

It would be such a fine opportunity, Mother rcmarked, to use the beautiful new china and all their nice silver.

After some discussion and deliberation, it was decided

194

to make the affair a whist party, and they might vary the evening with some musical selections. Maud, of course, would play, and she and Emily might render a few duets—"Invitation to the Waltz" they did particularly well, we thought. So it was all settled the list of guests made out, and Mother and Aunt Emily wrote the invitations.

There were the McAlisters, of course, Captain and Mrs. Hardy, the Howards, the Hales, Miss Lizzie Dexter, Cousin Ellen and a few of Father's associates—one a very grand person, an Austrian lawyer who wore very distinguished-looking brown whiskers, silky as a baby's hair, and had large, very white teeth and melancholy, dark eyes. Moreover, he was young, that is, fairly young, which lent an unusual thrill to the party for my sisters.

The parlors, in their new wallpaper, looked very grand and as the evenings had begun to grow cool, anthracite coal fires were lighted in the fireplaces and sent their cheer into every corner. Flowers, beautifully arranged by Miss Dexter, who came early to add her artistic last-minute touches, were set about in conspicuous places. Emil filled the lamps in the crystal chandeliers, trimmed the wicks, and lighted them, and in the soft glow our parlors looked so magnificent I could scarcely believe they were the same rooms in which we all sat quietly reading on Sunday afternoons. They reminded me of palaces I had read about in the Arabian Nights.

Days of excitement and happy toil had preceded this wonderful evening—hours in the genial kitchen, in which everyone who could wield a spoon or grease a pan was kept as busy as a bee. The best fowls in our flock had given up their lives in order that our chicken salad might be the very quintessence of chicken salad; old Alice had been fed to within an inch of her life so that she might furnish even richer milk and cream for the party; Emil and Anna had polished and scoured and cleaned untiringly, and every evening for a week the Democrat wagon turning in at our lane had been so laden with demijohns, cases, packages, and bags as completely to hide Father.

Uncle George took to the hayloft to compose a suitable poem of congratulations which he planned to read at the supper table on the great night. Aunt Emily made the Princess Louise Cake and Emily and Maud their Harlequin, Fig, Devil's Food, and I cannot recall how many other kinds and descriptions of cakes, sedulously practicing their duet betweenwhiles. It was a bewildering, amazing time, the most thrilling, I think, of my life, and although it had been decreed that Kitty and I, being only little girls, must not appear at the party, but go to bed at nine o'clock as usual, like good children, I felt that, after all, one can stand just so much happiness, and I had really had more than my share during the busy days of preparation.

But when the night actually arrived, Mother softened a bit, and we were permitted to station ourselves on the side veranda where, through the windows, we could watch the ladies as they came down the stairs after titivating at Mother's bedroom mirror. I wish I could remember what each one wore, for they presented such a kaleidoscopic effect of color, such silvery brilliance, such elegance and beauty, that my young eyes were fairly dazzled with their gorgeousness. Only a few stand out in my memory now—Kate McAlister in corn-colored silk with purple velvet trimmings, which seemed to contrast well with her jet-black hair; little Mrs. Hale in a fairylike dress of baby blue with flutings of white lace; Mother in her wedding gown of striped silk, a little tight perhaps, but beautiful; Miss Lizzie Dexter in delicate mauve with innumerable rows of fringe—they all looked magnificent to Kitty and me. But Aunt Emily—Aunt Emily—I had to look several times as she came tripping down the stairs before I recognized her—Aunt Emily in a shining satin dress of a brand-new fashionable color, "dregs of wine," and made with a train, the only train at the party, very tiny at the waist but not as tiny as Miss Lizzie Dexter, and—with a low neck! Her hair was done in a pompadour, the first we had ever seen, and I think the first, perhaps, in Chicago (although this new style in hairdressing was being much discussed), and a little bunch of dregs-of-wine ostrich tips was set coquettishly at the side as though to call attention to the pompadour. But nothing at all was needed to call attention to the low neck. Aunt Emily looked very handsome, I had to admit to myself, but I am sure a good many shivers of disapproval ran up and down a good many backs at the sight of that low-cut gown, as she floated into the parlor. However, Aunt Emily seemed quite unconcerned.

More shivers ran up and down more backs, I am sure, when the Austrian lawyer kissed her hand, as he was introduced, but Aunt Emily never even blushed; in fact, she acted as though a kiss on the finger tips was quite as ordinary a manner of greeting as a handshake.

I was terribly worried, for I wanted our nice Aunt Emily to make a good impression on our friends, and I feared she wasn't going to, so I went around by the garden walk to the kitchen door and into the dining room to be cheered by the grandeur of the table.

The Princess Louise Cake had the place of honor in the very center, its glistening tiers standing inches above everything else; silver epergnes of fruit, beautifully and regularly arranged, flanked it on either side; and glass dishes of Mother's pickled olives and other dainties were placed here and there. The lovely china, the cut-glass tumblers that rang like a bell if you so much as touched them, and the very best silver knives and forks and spoons were laid out in imposing array at each place. On the sideboard were more cakes, the silver coffee service, and the champagne glasses.

Back to the kitchen I went, to find Anna and Emil busy with the substantial things of the feast. The chicken salad was mounded to a peak, trimmed with rows of capers and topped with a bouquet of celery leaves. There was to be a hot dish, too, of some kind; it was now under way, and pans of Mother's best rolls, made small and elegant, were waiting to be put into the oven at the proper moment. In the milk room, where it would keep cool and fresh, one of Aunt Sophie's Tipsy Parsons, with cubes of red jelly decorating it, reposed in our largest and handsomest glass dish; and in the milk room, too, packed in buckets of ice, was the champagne.

It all looked so wonderful, so splendid, I could not tear myself away, although Anna tried to bribe me with a bunch of white grapes and two little cakes, to follow Kitty, who had already gone placidly to bed. But Kitty was always a good little girl, never greedy never disobedient, always meekly demure and submissive. I was of different stuff, impulsive, itching to be in everything, too often, I fear, unbearably inquisitive. How could I go calmly to sleep when so many exciting, delightful things were going on right in my own home?

I ate the grapes and the cakes, of course, and then I remembered *Jane Eyre*, a book I had been reading only in stolen moments, my parents considering it far too old and sophisticated for a girl of my tender age, but here was an opportunity to go on with the story. Would Jane marry Mr. Rochester, or would she not? I had left her in such an undecided frame of mind at my last hurried reading.

So, slipping the book from the shelf by Maud's bed, I hurried with it to the attic, our sanctuary and refuge in all times of need, garbed myself in a warm but very much outgrown nightgown of canton flannel, abstracted a few candle ends and matches from Molly's secret hiding place, and crawled under the bed with my precious prize, settling myself on my stomach for an hour or two of luxurious enjoyment. It was cozy under the bed, cozy and warm. My nightgown, though old and buttonless protected me from the cold, and the sound of the "Invitation to the Waltz" floating up to me from the parlor, prevented any feeling of loneliness and isolation I might have experienced. I was absorbed in Jane's romantic love affair with the stern Mr. Rochester.

I read on and on. It was fun at first with the candle spluttering beside me, fun until I reached the description of Jane's fright as she watched Mr. Rochester's maniacal wife tear the wedding veil asunder:

"Fearful and ghastly—the roll of the red eyes—the fearful blackened inflation of the lineaments—lips swelled and dark, like a foul vampire."

The burning words brought to my mind every ghost story I had ever read. I shivered with cold and terror. Near the bed under which I was cowering was a cracked looking glass on which my candle sent a flickering light. I thought I could discern in it the reflection of a moving figure. That there were weird sounds somewhere in the attic, and uncanny breezes blowing, I was certain, but for some minutes I was too terrified to move.

Then, because I could bear the strain no longer, I scrambled from my retreat and ran shrieking through the house, *Jane Eyre* in one hand, the lighted candle in the other, convinced that something horrid was after me—I could even feel its ghoulish hands touch me as I fled. Slamming doors behind me I scurried down the stairs, through the hall, as fast as my robust legs could take me, my face streaming with tears and my pigtails flying. Into the very dining room itself I went, where the guests, all looking so genteel and aristocratic, had just risen in response to Uncle

George's poem to toast Mother and Father in the unwonted champagne. It was just like a picture, but I did not stop to admire it. I flew, sobbing and shrieking, to Mother, and she, shamefaced at the spectacle I presented, drew me to her and tried to hush my bellowing and at the same time to cover my fat legs with my too short nightgown.

What a commotion! Champagne glasses fell to the floor, spilling their contents on beautiful dresses as they shattered. Ladies added their fluttering squeaks to my lusty howls. Mother's face was scarlet, Father's ominously white. Suddenly he rose, took *Jane Eyre* from me, seized my quaking arm, and led me, still sobbing, from the room into the parlor, straight to the fireplace.

Oh, I knew what was going to happen then! Had he not once thrown *Lady Audley's Secret* down the well? And sure enough, before I could protest, *Jane Eyre* was shriveling on the red coals—Mr. Rochester's fervent words and Jane's meek replies curling into ashes.

Stonily Father watched the holocaust. I watched it with anguish. Finally Father turned his eyes distastefully on me, took in my abbreviated, buttonless nightgown, my husky red knees, my untidy head, and, I hoped, my pleading glance, then he said icily,

"You have disgraced your mother and me, Miss." (Only when he was very angry or about to pass some dire judgment on us did he so address his daughters.) "You have seen fit to select an occasion like this to bitterly disappoint and shame us. For the next year, Miss, you will read nothing but cookbooks, and do not let me hear of your disobeying my commands."

"No, Father," I replied humbly.

And that mandate of Father's marked the beginning of my career.

About the Recipes

"A good recipe, for modern convenience," writes M.F.K. Fisher in *With Bold Knife and Fork* "should consist of three parts: name, ingredients, method. The first will perforce give some sort of description: for instance, one does not simply say 'Cake' or 'Bread,' but 'Golden Sponge Cake,' or 'Greek Honey Bread.' The ingredients should be listed in one column or two, rather than in a running sentence, according to the order of their use, and with the exact amount of each ingredient given before its name. The method should in most cases tell the temperature of the oven first, if one is needed . . . ." None of the recipes in *Victorian Cakes* entirely fulfill the standards set by Mrs. Fisher; nevertheless, they are delicious reading in themselves and do produce creditable results if they are carefully read and interpreted before any cake-making is begun.

Victorian cakes, in general, were richer than cakes popular today. Although modern tasters might unkindly describe many Victorian cakes as heavy, the buttery, eggy, milky quality of their crumb attests to the good honest ingredients they contain. I have tested all the recipes, and the following information will help insure success.

201

VICTORIAN CAKES

Ingredients

FLOUR

Mrs. King explains that "we had but one grade of flour and that was always selected for its bread qualities." Recipes for the lighter, more delicate cakes call for part flour, part cornstarch. All the recipes in the book were tested with good results using unbleached all-purpose flour.

SUGAR

Sugar crystals were much coarser at the end of the nineteenth century than they are today, and a greater amount of sugar was required for sweetening purposes. Sugar has the ability to soften or dissolve the gluten in flour and, when combined with other ingredients such as butter, it helps produce a tender cake. A larger quantity of sugar than we are used to today was needed to counteract the high amount of gluten in the bread flour that was considered "all-purpose" flour in most Victorian households. In the recipes calling for two or more cups sugar, the amount of sugar can be reduced by ½ cup without noticeably affecting the texture of the cake.

BUTTER

Washing the salt from butter is mentioned more than once in *Victorian Cakes*. In the testing of the recipes, unsalted butter was used exclusively for its fresh, clean taste. It was also used in place of lard in the few recipes which specified that ingredient: today's lard purchased at the supermarket is very different in texture and taste from the home-rendered product of a century ago.

DRIED FRUITS AND NUTS

Dark raisins, golden Sultana raisins ("raisins of the

sun") and currants were favored additions to many Victorian cakes. In the 1880s, dark raisins were the dried fruits of the large seeded Muscat grape. Before they could be baked in a cake, Muscat raisins had to be cut open and the seeds removed. The raisins were then halved or sliced.

The seedless varieties of raisins we have today make seeding and slicing unnecessary. (If the seeded Muscat raisins are available, they are worth the extra work, for their flavor is superb.) Many of the recipes in this book call for well-washed currants: washing currants is another unnecessary chore as currants are now cleaned before they are packaged. Both raisins and currants are improved if steamed over water or plumped in a little orange juice or brandy before they are used.

Candied lemon and orange peel and citron were common ingredients in the nineteenth-century kitchen. Candied peels and fruits manufactured today are usually heavily coated with preservatives, and it is necessary to wash these ingredients before using them. In a bowl, pour boiling water to cover over the required amount of candied fruit, stirring and swishing the water for about a minute. Rinse and drain the fruit thoroughly before using it. Soaking the fruit in sherry or Madeira for a few hours improves its flavor immensely.

Nowadays, the citron sold in America is the candied rind of the *Citrullus* melon, but in Victorian times, it was the whole candied fruit of the *Citrus medica*, a type of citrus tree. The recipes in *Victorian Cakes* which call for citron specify that it be shaved or finely shaved; this was done laboriously by hand, with a heavy, sharp knife. The easiest way to treat citron—and candied lemon and orange peel— is to drop the fruit into a blender or through the feed tube of a food processor with the motor running and chop it fine.

Hickory nuts, called for in two recipes, are hard to come by and even harder to shell: it is almost impossible to crack the tiny nutshells without breaking the nutmeats inside into bits and pieces. Substituting pecans for the hickory nuts in the Hickory Nut Cake is perfectly legitimate, as pecans are a variety of this native American nut. Likewise, pecans may be substituted for the hickory nuts in the Pork Cake.

Oven Temperatures

In Victorian times, oven temperatures were gauged by the number of seconds a housewife could comfortably hold her hand inside a preheated oven or, as *The Rumford Almanac Cookbook of 1888* suggests, by throwing a handful of flour on the floor of the oven and counting the seconds it takes to brown. Oven thermometers were kitchen tools of the future.

A "moderate" oven, 350 degrees Fahrenheit, is most often requested in the recipes in this book; it is also the correct temperature to use when a recipe does not give any indication of how hot the oven should be. The oven temperatures in the recipes are as follows:

	Degrees Fahrenheit	Degrees Celsius
Barely warm, cool (for the jelly kisses)	275	135
Slow	300	150
Very Moderate	325	165
Moderate	350	180
Moderately hot	375	190
Hot	400	205

Baking Pans

It was not until the nineteenth century that cakes were baked in layers. A "loaf" cake traditionally referred to any solid, unlayered cake, whether baked in a rectangular, cylindrical or round tube pan. In *Victorian Cakes*, a loaf

pan or loaf-cake pan is specified in many of the recipes—
Applesauce Cake, for example, is baked in a square loaf
pan, and Blackberry Cake in a shallow loaf-cake pan. The
layer cakes call for typical, round layer cake pans or shallow rectangular pans. Round pans 8½ to 9½ inches in
diameter were used with good results in the testing of the
recipes; so were rectangular pans 12- by 8-inches and at
least 1½ inches deep.

Icings

Nineteenth-century cake embellishments included in
the basic sugar-with-cream, fruit juice or water icing, as
well as a simple brown-sugar and sour-cream icing.
Emily's cakes were usually iced with uncooked egg-white
icing, "merely egg white, a little cold water, fine sugar,
much beating, and as an aristocratic touch, a few drops,
only a few, mind, of some fragrant, delicate extract." To
the modern palate, this icing is overly sweet and sticky and
tastes of raw egg. Boiled icing, another nineteenth-century
favorite, is also very sweet. Meringue buttercream, a varia-
tion of boiled icing, is less sweet, and is creamy rather than
sticky.

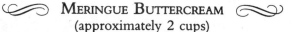

MERINGUE BUTTERCREAM
(approximately 2 cups)

1 cup sugar	½ cup water
3 egg whites	A pinch of cream of tartar
1 cup (2 sticks) unsalted butter, softened	Flavoring as desired

In a saucepan over low heat, combine the sugar and
water. Stir until the sugar is completely dissolved. Raise
the heat, and when the syrup comes to a boil, cover the
saucepan for 2 minutes. Uncover and continue to let the
syrup boil without stirring, until the temperature reaches
238° F on a candy thermometer—or until a few drops of

syrup form a soft ball in cold water.

While the syrup is cooking, beat the egg whites with the cream of tartar until they form stiff peaks.

Beating the egg whites moderately slowly, pour in the sugar syrup in a thin stream. Continue beating at high speed until the mixture is cool. It will be shiny, smooth and quite stiff.

Beat the softened butter into the meringue mixture. Continue beating until the buttercream is completely smooth. If it is too soft to spread, refrigerate until firm, then beat again until smooth. Flavor the buttercream with melted chocolate or cocoa, sherry, Madeira, instant coffee dissolved in a little water, or lemon, orange or almond extract.

Basic buttercream is another icing that would have found favor in the Campion household.

⮞ BASIC BUTTERCREAM ICING ⮜
(approximately 2 cups)

¾ cups (1½ sticks) unsalted butter, softened	4 cups powdered sugar 4 tablespoons cream Flavoring as desired

Beat the butter until it is light and fluffy. Gradually beat the sugar into the butter, alternating with the cream, until the mixture is smooth. Beat in the flavoring. If the icing is too thick, beat in a little more cream; if it is too thin, add a little more sugar.

Of all the recipes in this book only two needed to be adapted "for modern convenience." The recipe for Bread Cake on page 52 calls for the amount of dough "as would comfortably fill our old cracked coffee cup, pressed down and running over"—not very precise! The recipe for

Shrewsbury Cakes on page 70 requires 12 cups of flour and "butter to make a proper paste." This amount of dough "rolled thin as paper" would produce at least a thousand of the scalloped cookies. The adapted recipes follow:

⎰⎱ BREAD CAKE ⎰⎱
(3 loaves)

1 cake yeast, crumbled	½ teaspoon cinnamon
½ cup sugar	½ teaspoon mace
1¼ cups tepid water	2 tablespoons finely
5½ cups flour, plus a	chopped candied citron
few tablespoons more,	2 tablespoons finely
if necessary	chopped lemon peel
1 teaspoon salt	2 tablespoons finely
¾ cup (1½ sticks)	chopped orange peel
unsalted butter, softened	¾ cup currants
4 eggs	¾ cup Sultana raisins
½ teaspoon nutmeg	

In a large bowl combine the yeast and 1 tablespoon of the sugar with ¼ cup of the water. Stir gently and let sit a few minutes until the mixture is thick and creamy. Pour the rest of the tepid water into the bowl and add the salt, stirring to dissolve. Add 3½ cups of flour, one cup at a time, mixing well after each addition. When the mixture has formed a ball, turn it out onto a well-floured surface. Knead the dough, adding a little more flour, if necessary, until it is elastic and no longer sticky—about 10 minutes. Shape the dough into a ball.

Butter a large bowl and place the ball of dough in the bowl, turning it several times to coat the surface with butter. Cover the bowl with plastic wrap and let the dough rise until it has doubled in volume—about 1 to 1½ hours. While the dough is rising, cream together the butter and sugar. In another bowl, beat the eggs with the spices.

Punch down the risen dough and, using your hands, gradually work in the butter-sugar mixture, and then the beaten eggs. Work in the remaining 2 cups of flour and the candied fruits, currants, and Sultanas. The dough will be very heavy.

Divide the dough into three equal parts. Shape into 3 loaves and put into 3 well-buttered 8-inch loaf pans. The pans should be no more than half full. Cover and let rise until the loaves have doubled in size—about 1 hour. Pre-heat the oven to 350° F.

Bake the bread cakes in the preheated oven for about 1 hour, or until they are golden brown. Remove the cakes from the pans, rub them all over with butter and let them cool wrapped in a towel.

∽ SHREWSBURY CAKES ∾
(30 cookies)

2½ cups flour, plus a few tablespoons more, if necessary	½ cup sugar
	1 egg, well beaten
½ teaspoon cinnamon	¼ teaspoon rosewater
½ teaspoon nutmeg	1 cup (2 sticks) unsalted butter, melted

Into a mixing bowl, sift together the flour, cinnamon and nutmeg. Mix in the sugar, egg and rosewater. Gradually stir in the butter. Turn the dough out onto a floured surface and knead for a few minutes, adding a little more flour if the dough is too soft to roll. Preheat the oven to 350° F.

Roll the dough as thin as possible and cut it with a scalloped cookie cutter. Place cookies on buttered baking sheets and bake for 10 minutes, or until golden.

NOTE: Nut pieces or caraway seeds may be pressed into the surface of the cookies before they are baked. They also may be sprinkled with sugar before baking.

Jill Gardner